RJ STARR

The Architecture of Being Human

A Structural Framework for Understanding Mind, Emotion, Identity, and Meaning

Depthmark

Psychological Architecture is the study of how mind, emotion, identity, and meaning form the structural system through which human experience is organized.

- RJ Starr

Contents

Introduction

Why Understanding the Structure of the Mind Matters

Human beings move through their lives guided by interpretations they rarely notice. A comment from a colleague lingers longer than expected. A passing disappointment colors the mood of an entire afternoon. A decision that once seemed obvious begins to feel uncertain months later. Thoughts arise, emotions shift, memories return, identities evolve, and meanings gradually take shape as life unfolds. Beneath these ordinary moments lies a quiet structure organizing how experience is interpreted, how emotions signal significance, how identity holds a life together, and how meaning gives direction to the future. Most people live within this structure without ever seeing it.

Yet most people rarely pause to ask a deeper question: what kind of system organizes these experiences in the first place?

We tend to notice the content of psychological life rather than the structure that produces it. We notice what we feel in a particular moment. We notice the beliefs we hold about ourselves. We notice the hopes we carry, the worries that occupy the mind, and the emotions that move through our days. These experiences feel personal and immediate, and because they are so familiar, they often appear to arise naturally, as if they simply occur on their own.

But beneath this flow of experience lies a deeper organizing system.

The thoughts that pass through the mind, the emotional responses that follow events, the sense of identity that develops over years, and the meanings individuals construct about their lives do not appear randomly. They emerge through a structured psychological system that quietly organizes how human experience unfolds.

This book refers to that system as Psychological Architecture.

Psychological Architecture describes the structural organization of human experience. It proposes that psychological life is composed of four interacting domains: mind, emotion, identity, and meaning. Each domain plays a distinct role within the overall system, yet none operates independently. Together they form the architecture through which individuals interpret events, regulate emotional responses, maintain a sense of self, and situate their lives within a broader framework of significance.

Understanding this architecture requires a shift in perspective.

Psychology is often approached through the study of individual phenomena: behaviors, symptoms, personality traits, emotional states, or cognitive biases. These approaches can yield valuable insights, but they often examine psychological events in isolation. They describe what people think or feel without fully explaining how these experiences are organized within a larger system.

A structural perspective asks a different question.

Rather than focusing only on isolated thoughts or emotions, it asks how the system itself is organized. How do interpretive processes shape perception? How are emotional responses regulated? How does identity maintain continuity across time? Through what structures do individuals construct meaning from the events of their lives?

Seen from this vantage point, many familiar psychological experiences begin to appear in a different light. Emotional reactivity, persistent rumination, identity conflict, existential uncertainty, and patterns of avoidance are rarely isolated occurrences. They are often expressions of deeper dynamics within the psychological system. When the underlying architecture becomes strained or unstable, the effects appear across multiple domains of experience.

This is not unique to psychology. In many fields, understanding a complex phenomenon requires examining the structure beneath the surface.

A physician studying symptoms considers the physiological systems that produce them. An engineer investigating a malfunction examines the structure of the machine rather than the visible problem alone. An urban planner studying the activity of a city must understand the infrastructure that organizes movement through its streets.

Human experience operates in a similar way.

The thoughts people have, the emotions they feel, the identities they construct, and the meanings they pursue do not arise independently. They emerge from interactions within a broader psychological architecture.

One way to understand this relationship is through an analogy to language.

When we listen to someone speak, we hear words arranged into sentences. The meaning of those sentences appears immediately to the listener. Yet the ability to produce coherent language depends on an underlying grammatical structure. Grammar organizes language in ways that often remain invisible to the people using it. Without grammar, words would still exist, but meaningful communication would collapse.

Psychological experience functions in a similar manner.

The visible elements of experience—thoughts, emotions, beliefs, memories, and narratives—resemble the words of psychological life. The architecture beneath them functions like grammar, organizing how these elements combine into meaningful patterns. Without recognizing that structure, we may observe the content of experience without understanding the system that produces it.

Psychological Architecture attempts to make that structure visible.

At the center of this framework are four domains that together organize the system of human experience.

The first domain is mind. The mind functions as the interpretive engine of the psychological system. Human perception is not a passive recording of events. The mind continuously interprets incoming information, organizes patterns, constructs explanations, and generates expectations about what events mean. Through these interpretive processes, individuals create a coherent representation of the world around them.

The second domain is emotion. Emotion functions as the regulatory system of the architecture. Emotional processes signal what matters. They highlight potential threats, indicate safety or attachment, and register experiences of loss, connection, satisfaction, or distress. In doing so, emotion guides attention and motivates action.

The third domain is identity. Identity provides continuity within the psychological system. It organizes the narrative through which individuals understand who they are across time. Identity integrates memories, roles, values, relationships, and self-perceptions into a relatively stable framework that anchors experience.

The fourth domain is meaning. Meaning functions as the integrative structure of the architecture. It allows individuals to situate their lives within broader frameworks of purpose, value, and existential understanding. Where identity organizes the story of the self, meaning situates that story within a larger horizon of significance.

These four domains interact continuously.

Interpretations generated by the mind influence emotional responses. Emotional experiences shape identity narratives. Identity affects how events are interpreted and how emotional reactions are processed. Meaning provides the wider context through which identity, emotion, and interpretation are integrated into a coherent understanding of life.

Because these domains operate simultaneously, psychological stability depends on their interaction. When the domains remain relatively aligned, individuals often experience a sense of coherence. Interpretation, emotion, identity, and meaning reinforce one another, allowing life to unfold within a stable psychological framework.

However, when tensions arise between these domains, the architecture of experience can begin to strain. Interpretive patterns may intensify emotional responses. Emotional regulation may become unstable under prolonged stress. Identity narratives may fracture under conflicting pressures. Meaning frameworks may weaken during periods of loss, transition, or existential uncertainty.

When these dynamics interact, the psychological system can begin to destabilize. What initially appears as an isolated emotional difficulty or cognitive pattern may reflect deeper structural tensions across the architecture.

A structural perspective allows these patterns to be examined more clearly.

Instead of focusing only on individual thoughts or emotional reactions, it becomes possible to observe how the system itself is functioning. Interpretive patterns, emotional regulation, identity organization, and meaning structures can be understood as interconnected elements of a larger psychological system.

The perspective developed in this book draws on several intellectual traditions within the history of psychological thought. Cognitive psychology has explored how interpretive processes shape perception and understanding. Affective science has examined the regulatory role of emotional systems. Developmental psychology has studied how identity forms across the lifespan. Existential psychology has explored the human search for meaning within conditions of uncertainty, freedom, and responsibility.

Systems theory has also influenced this framework. Systems theory emphasizes that complex phenomena often arise from interactions among multiple components rather than from any single element operating alone. Applied to psychology, this perspective encourages us to view human experience as the product of interacting domains rather than isolated mechanisms.

Psychological Architecture integrates insights from these traditions into a unified structural perspective. Psychological Architecture does not replace these traditions. It builds upon them. Cognitive psychology has clarified the interpretive processes through which the mind organizes perception and understanding. Affective science has explored the regulatory role of emotional systems in guiding attention and behavior. Developmental psychology has examined the formation of identity across the lifespan, while existential psychology has investigated the human search for meaning under conditions of freedom, responsibility, and uncertainty. Systems theory contributes the insight that complex outcomes often emerge from interactions among multiple components rather than from isolated mechanisms. Psychological Architecture brings these strands together within a single structural perspective, examining how interpretation, emotion, identity, and meaning operate as interacting domains within the organization of human experience.

Later in the book, this architectural perspective will be explored through a series of structural models that illuminate recurring patterns within the system. These include the Emotional Avoidance Loop, the Identity Collapse Cycle, the Self-Perception Map, the Emotional Maturity Index, and Emotional Repatterning. These models function as analytical lenses that reveal how the domains of mind, emotion, identity, and meaning interact to produce recognizable patterns of experience.

By examining these patterns, it becomes possible to observe how psychological systems maintain stability, how they become strained under pressure, and how structural reorganization may occur over time.

Human experience is extraordinarily complex, and no single framework can capture every dimension of psychological life. The purpose of this book is therefore not to provide definitive answers to every psychological question. Instead, it offers a way of seeing.

Much of the architecture that shapes experience operates outside conscious awareness. Interpretive patterns become habitual. Emotional responses consolidate across years of experience. Identity narratives develop gradually through relationships and life transitions. Meaning structures deepen through reflection on responsibility, loss, and possibility.

Because these processes unfold slowly and often invisibly, the architecture guiding experience may remain unnoticed.

Yet it is always present.

It shapes how events are interpreted, how emotions are regulated, how identities are maintained, and how meaning emerges from the unfolding story of a life.

To study psychology without examining this structure would be similar to studying language without considering grammar. The words of experience may be visible, but the system organizing them remains unseen.

The study of Psychological Architecture begins by bringing that structure into view.

By examining the interacting domains of mind, emotion, identity, and meaning, we begin to see the architecture through which human experience is organized. Understanding that architecture allows us to observe psychological life with greater clarity, revealing the structural patterns that shape how individuals navigate the complexities of being human.

Scope of the Framework

The framework presented in this book is not intended to replace existing psychological theories or research traditions. Psychology has developed a vast body of knowledge across cognitive science, affective science, developmental psychology, social psychology, and existential inquiry. Each of these fields illuminates important aspects of human experience. Psychological Architecture approaches this body of knowledge from a different vantage point. Rather than focusing on individual psychological phenomena in isolation, it examines how several core domains of experience—interpretation, emotion, identity, and meaning—interact to form the structural organization through which psychological life unfolds. The goal of the framework is therefore integrative rather than replacement. It offers a way of seeing how multiple strands of psychological insight may be understood within a coherent system.

* * *

1

The Hidden Structures of Human Experience

Human beings live inside a continuous flow of psychological experience. Thoughts arise in response to events. Emotions shift as circumstances change. Memories return, sometimes with startling force. Expectations about the future form almost automatically. Interpretations appear so quickly that they often feel less like interpretations than like reality itself. From the inside, this movement of thought and feeling seems natural. It feels like life simply unfolding.

Because this process is so constant, most people rarely stop to examine it. They notice what they are thinking, what they are feeling, what they are worried about, what they hope will happen, what they regret, what they want. They notice the content of experience. Much less often do they pause to ask what organizes that content in the first place.

That question matters more than it first appears.

The patterns that define a human life are not simply random collections of thoughts, emotions, and reactions. They are not isolated mental events floating freely through consciousness. Human experience takes shape through an underlying organization. There is a structure to the way perception becomes interpretation, the way interpretation becomes emotional significance, the way repeated experiences become part of identity, and the way identity becomes linked to larger questions of purpose, direction, and meaning.

Most of the time, this structure remains hidden. People feel the consequences of it without seeing it directly. They know what it is like to become anxious before a difficult conversation, to replay a moment of embarrassment long after it has ended, to feel destabilized by failure, to wonder whether they are becoming someone different from the person they thought they were, or to find themselves asking what any of it means after a loss or major transition. These experiences are familiar. Yet they are often encountered as isolated episodes rather than as expressions of a larger system.

This book begins from the idea that human beings live inside such a system whether they recognize it or not.

The thoughts people have, the emotions they struggle to regulate, the identities they construct, and the meanings they pursue are not separate psychological curiosities. They are interacting dimensions of a broader architecture. What appears on the surface as a passing thought or a momentary emotional reaction may reflect deeper patterns within the structure of the mind. What looks like confusion in one area of life may actually involve tensions distributed across several domains at once.

To see this clearly requires a change in perspective. Instead of asking only what a person feels, thinks, or does in a given moment, it becomes necessary to ask how the system itself is organized. What kind of structure produces these recurring experiences? How do perception, feeling, self-understanding, and purpose become woven together into a recognizable human life? Why do some experiences destabilize the whole system while others are absorbed and integrated without lasting disruption?

These are structural questions. They move beneath the immediate contents of consciousness and toward the organization that makes those contents possible.

This does not mean reducing psychological life to something mechanical. Human beings are not machines, and the architecture described in this book is not a rigid blueprint imposed on experience from the outside. It is a living structure, one that develops across time, responds to relationships and circumstance, and remains shaped by history, culture, memory, and vulnerability. But precisely because human experience is so complex, it cannot be understood well through fragments alone. A more integrated perspective is needed.

That perspective begins with a simple but easily overlooked recognition: human beings are always living inside systems they do not fully see.

Living Inside Systems We Rarely See

In ordinary life, people move through complex systems without much awareness of the structures supporting them. A person can live in a city for decades without understanding how its water is routed, how its electrical grid functions, or how transportation networks shape the movement of daily life. Most of the time, those systems remain invisible because they are working. Only when something fails does the hidden infrastructure become visible. A blackout reveals the grid. A transit breakdown reveals the network. An interruption exposes the structure that was quietly organizing life all along.

Something similar is true of psychological experience.

Human beings live within systems of interpretation, emotional regulation, identity organization, and meaning-making that shape their experience continuously. These systems determine what gets noticed, what feels threatening, what seems possible, what becomes memorable, what fits into the story of the self, and what appears worthwhile or empty. Yet because these processes operate continuously and often beneath awareness, they rarely present themselves as systems. They appear instead as life itself.

A person notices that they feel tense in certain conversations but may not notice the interpretive expectations already active before the conversation begins. Another person finds themselves repeatedly drawn to approval, success, or reassurance without seeing the deeper identity structure that gives these experiences such significance. Someone else feels lost after a divorce, a career collapse, or the death of a parent and experiences that loss not only as pain but as a disruption in orientation, as though the very map of life has changed. In each case, the visible experience is real. But the visible experience is not the whole story. Something deeper is organizing it.

One reason this deeper organization is hard to see is that psychological systems are lived from the inside. A person does not stand outside their own mind and observe it objectively the way an engineer might examine a bridge. They are immersed in it. Their interpretations are already shaping what they see. Their emotions are already directing attention. Their identity is already influencing what feels personally threatening or affirming. Their framework of meaning is already influencing whether a setback appears tolerable, devastating, instructive, unfair, or absurd.

Because of this, individuals often misrecognize structural patterns as isolated episodes. They think they have a problem with overthinking, with sensitivity, with confidence, with motivation, with attachment, with anger, with emptiness. Sometimes those descriptions capture part of what is happening. But often they are surface-level labels placed on deeper structural dynamics.

Consider a simple social example. Two people leave the same conversation with entirely different impressions of what just occurred. One feels dismissed and unsettled. The other feels the discussion was neutral and brief. The difference may not lie only in what was said. It may also lie in how each person's interpretive habits, emotional sensitivities, identity concerns, and prior expectations organized the experience. The external event was shared, but the psychological event was not. Each person inhabited a different version of its significance.

Or consider the experience of waiting for a text message that never arrives. On the surface, this may seem trivial. But psychologically it can activate an entire system. One person shrugs and assumes the other is busy. Another becomes preoccupied, then anxious, then self-critical, then resentful. What changed was not simply the absence of a message. What changed was the interaction between interpretation, emotional regulation, identity narrative, and meaning. The event became structurally amplified.

Most people have had some version of this experience. A moment that appears small on the outside acquires disproportionate weight on the inside. A remark, a silence, a missed opportunity, an expression on someone's face, a shift in tone. These moments are not psychologically powerful only because of what they are. They are powerful because of the system into which they enter.

This is one reason structural understanding matters. Without it, human experience can appear strangely chaotic. People seem inconsistent even to themselves. They may understand one part of what is happening while remaining confused about the rest. They may know that their reaction is larger than the moment seems to justify, yet still feel unable to regulate it. They may recognize that a certain pattern keeps recurring but not understand what sustains it. They feel the outcome without seeing the architecture that produces it.

A structural perspective changes the level of analysis. It asks not only what happened, but what kind of system made that event matter in this way. It asks not only what a person felt, but how that feeling was organized by interpretation, by prior learning, by self-structure, and by larger frameworks of significance. It does not deny the immediate reality of thought and emotion. It places them in context.

This shift is subtle but profound. Once people begin to understand themselves structurally, many experiences that once felt arbitrary begin to reveal pattern. Reactions become more intelligible. Repetition becomes easier to see. The psychological landscape begins to look less like a series of disconnected moments and more like an organized environment through which a person is moving.

That environment is not static. It develops. It absorbs experience. It becomes strained. It reorganizes under pressure. But it is not random. It has discernible forms, recurring tensions, and identifiable domains. The challenge is that modern life does not naturally teach people to see this level of structure. It teaches them to respond to symptoms, episodes, traits, and visible behaviors. It gives names to parts. It does not always show how the parts belong to a system.

This helps explain why even sophisticated psychological language can leave people feeling only partially understood. They may acquire a label for what they feel without gaining a clearer map of why those feelings interact with identity, thought, and meaning in the way they do. They gain vocabulary, but not architecture.

To move beyond that limitation, it is necessary to examine a broader problem in modern psychological understanding: fragmentation.

The Limits of Fragmented Psychology

Modern psychology has produced enormous insight into the workings of the human mind. It has studied attention, memory, cognition, attachment, affect, development, motivation, trauma, personality, social influence, and many other dimensions of human functioning. This body of knowledge is significant and indispensable. No serious effort to understand human beings can ignore it.

At the same time, the growth of psychological knowledge has often come through specialization. Different domains of inquiry developed their own methods, vocabularies, assumptions, and preferred problems. Cognitive psychology focused on mental processes. Affective science investigated emotion. Developmental psychology examined change across the lifespan. Social psychology studied group influence and interpersonal behavior. Personality theory pursued stable individual differences. Existential psychology engaged questions of freedom, mortality, anxiety, meaning, and responsibility. Clinical models focused on distress, dysfunction, diagnosis, and treatment.

Each of these domains has contributed something important. But when taken separately, they can produce an understanding of psychological life that feels partitioned. Thought is studied here, emotion there, identity somewhere else, meaning elsewhere still. Valuable insights emerge, yet the lived reality of human experience does not arrive in these compartments.

In actual life, a person does not first have a cognitive event, then an emotional event, then an identity event, then a meaning event, each in clean sequence. They experience all of these dimensions at once. A breakup is not merely emotional pain. It is interpretation, attachment, self-understanding, memory, anticipated future, and often a crisis of meaning. Career failure is not simply disappointment. It may also destabilize identity, distort interpretation, alter emotional regulation, and change a person's sense of purpose. Grief is never just sadness. It is also altered structure. The world no longer means what it meant before.

Fragmented psychology can describe pieces of these processes well, yet still miss the form of the whole.

This becomes especially clear in the way psychological language is used publicly. A person may be told they are struggling with anxiety, cognitive distortions, low self-esteem, emotional dysregulation, poor boundaries, insecure attachment, or an identity crisis. Each of these descriptions may contain truth. Yet in many cases they remain conceptually adjacent rather than structurally integrated. They describe important features of experience without fully clarifying how those features are interacting inside a single system.

The result is a common kind of psychological partial understanding. People know a great deal about isolated concepts while still feeling uncertain about their own overall organization. They understand traits without structure. They understand symptoms without system. They understand episodes without architecture.

This fragmentation also affects how people imagine change. If the problem is understood only as a faulty thought pattern, the solution appears to lie in correcting thought. If the problem is described only as emotional reactivity, the solution seems to lie in regulating feeling. If the problem is framed only as insecurity, then self-esteem becomes the target. But many forms of psychological distress are not problems in one isolated area. They are tensions distributed across several domains simultaneously. A person may reinterpret an event more rationally and still feel emotionally destabilized by it because the deeper issue involves identity threat. Another may learn self-soothing techniques yet remain disoriented because the more central crisis concerns meaning. Another may gain confidence and still remain vulnerable to collapse because their interpretive structure has not changed.

None of this means specialized psychology is wrong. It means specialization alone is insufficient.

To understand human experience more fully, it becomes necessary to reconnect the parts within a larger frame. This is where a structural perspective becomes useful. A structural perspective does not discard cognitive insight, emotional theory, developmental knowledge, or existential inquiry. Instead, it places them into relation. It asks how these dimensions operate together. It treats them not as competing explanations but as interacting domains within one psychological architecture.

This shift has several consequences.

First, it changes what counts as an explanation. Instead of asking only why a person feels anxious, it becomes possible to ask what interpretation is generating the anxiety, what identity concern is being activated, and what larger threat to orientation or meaning might be involved. Instead of asking only why a person feels stuck, it becomes possible to ask whether the problem lies in motivation, self-concept, emotional fear, or a broader collapse in purpose. Instead of viewing recurring patterns as disconnected failures, they can be understood as structurally coherent outcomes generated by the interaction of several forces at once.

Second, it changes how psychological stability is understood. Stability is no longer seen merely as the management of symptoms or the control of emotional states. It becomes a matter of alignment across domains. A person is more stable when interpretation, emotion, identity, and meaning are working in relative coordination. They become less stable when those domains begin to strain against one another.

Third, it changes how breakdown is understood. Structural breakdown rarely begins as total collapse. More often it begins as tension. Interpretations intensify. Emotion becomes harder to regulate. Identity grows brittle or uncertain. Meaning weakens. The person may initially experience these as separate problems. A structural view reveals them as interacting signs of destabilization within the same architecture.

This broader perspective is especially important for an entry-level framework book. If the reader is introduced only to pieces, the framework will feel like another collection of ideas. But if the reader begins to see how the pieces belong together, then a genuine shift in understanding becomes possible.

That shift is the real purpose of Psychological Architecture. It is not to add one more concept to the shelf. It is to offer a more coherent way of seeing psychological life itself.

To do that, the framework must begin at the level of structure.

Toward a Structural Understanding of the Mind

A structural understanding of psychological life begins with a different kind of question. Instead of asking only which trait, symptom, behavior, or mental process is present, it asks how the system itself is organized. What are the major domains through which human experience becomes coherent? How do they influence one another? What patterns emerge when they are aligned, and what forms of instability appear when they are not?

This is not a new impulse in human thought. In many fields, knowledge advances when attention shifts from isolated events to the systems generating them. Biology moved beyond the study of individual organs toward integrated understandings of the organism. Ecology made it impossible to understand a species apart from the larger environment in which it lives. Systems theory showed that many complex outcomes arise not from one component acting alone but from relationships among components.

Psychology is no exception. Human experience is too interdependent to be adequately understood in fragments. Thoughts shape feeling. Feeling shapes attention. Attention influences memory. Memory informs identity. Identity influences interpretation. Meaning gives broader significance to all of it. To isolate one domain completely from the others is to create explanatory convenience at the cost of lived reality.

A structural perspective attempts to repair this separation. It asks how experience is organized at a deeper level.

Within this perspective, the mind is not treated merely as a place where thoughts happen. It is treated as an interpretive system. Emotion is not treated merely as a disruptive force or subjective feeling-state. It is treated as a regulatory system that signals significance. Identity is not treated merely as a social label or personal preference. It is treated as the organizing narrative through which continuity is maintained. Meaning is not treated merely as inspiration or belief. It is treated as the integrative horizon that allows experience to feel situated within a larger whole.

These are not interchangeable functions. They represent distinct domains of psychological life. But neither are they independent. Their significance lies precisely in their interaction.

Interpretation shapes what feels threatening, promising, humiliating, hopeful, or unbearable. Emotional responses alter what receives attention and what becomes memorable. Identity determines what is taken personally, what confirms the self, and what endangers it. Meaning influences whether suffering appears pointless or endurable, whether sacrifice seems worth making, and whether a person can remain oriented through uncertainty.

Seen this way, human experience becomes more intelligible. A person is not simply overwhelmed. They may be interpreting events through threat, regulating emotion under strain, defending an identity structure, and losing contact with meaning all at once. Another is not merely unmotivated. They may be disconnected from significance, uncertain about self, emotionally flattened, and unable to interpret effort as worthwhile. Another is not only angry. They may be experiencing repeated identity threat filtered through an interpretive system that has become primed for violation and distrust.

A structural perspective allows these experiences to be understood as organized rather than random. This does not make them simple. It makes them legible.

It also makes room for development. Psychological architecture is not fixed. It is shaped across time. Early attachment, social environment, cultural values, repeated experiences of affirmation or threat, personal choices, loss, success, failure, and reflection all influence how the system develops. Interpretive tendencies can become more flexible or more rigid. Emotional regulation can strengthen or fray. Identity can broaden or become brittle. Meaning can deepen or collapse. The architecture changes, but it does not cease to be architecture. The very possibility of reorganization implies structure.

This matters because much of psychological life unfolds below explicit awareness. People do not usually announce to themselves that their interpretation is narrowing, that their identity is under strain, or that their meaning horizon has thinned. They feel the effects first. They notice anxiety, resentment, confusion, shame, emptiness, compulsion, exhaustion, or grief. Structural understanding helps connect these visible experiences to the hidden organization beneath them.

That is one of the central aims of this book. It is not to flatten complexity into slogans or to promise complete explanatory mastery over the human condition. No single framework can exhaust the richness of psychological life. Rather, the goal is to offer a way of seeing that makes human experience more coherent. The framework does not eliminate mystery. It clarifies structure.

This is especially important in an age saturated with psychological language but often lacking psychological integration. Many people have encountered enough concepts to describe parts of themselves, but not enough architecture to understand the relation among those parts. They know they are sensitive, avoidant, overthinking, emotionally reactive, driven, insecure, lonely, or burned out. What they often lack is a structural map showing how these experiences are linked.

A structural understanding of the mind begins to supply that map.

The Architecture of Human Experience

The framework developed in this book refers to the structural organization of psychological life as Psychological Architecture.

Psychological Architecture proposes that human experience is organized through four interacting domains: mind, emotion, identity, and meaning. These domains do not simply sit beside one another as separate topics. They function together as an architecture through which experience becomes organized, interpreted, regulated, narrated, and integrated across time.

The mind is the interpretive engine. It does not merely record reality as though it were a camera. It filters, selects, predicts, organizes, compares, and explains. It constructs a usable version of the world from incomplete information. Through the mind, events acquire shape and significance.

Emotion is the regulatory system. It signals what matters. It alerts, mobilizes, warns, attaches, grieves, and responds. Emotion is not merely something a person feels after interpretation has occurred. It operates in constant interaction with interpretation, helping determine what becomes salient, urgent, memorable, or difficult to ignore.

Identity is the organizing narrative. It gives continuity to experience by linking past, present, and anticipated future into a sense of self. Identity holds together roles, values, memories, loyalties, wounds, aspirations, and self-understandings. It answers, however imperfectly, the question of who a person takes themselves to be.

Meaning is the integrative structure. It situates personal life within broader frameworks of purpose, significance, value, responsibility, or existential orientation. Meaning is what allows suffering to be interpreted as bearable or unbearable, sacrifice as justified or futile, and life itself as coherent or fractured.

These four domains are analytically distinct, but lived experience rarely separates them cleanly. They are always interacting.

A thought is rarely just a thought. It carries emotional significance, fits or disrupts identity, and often draws its weight from a larger horizon of meaning. A feeling is rarely just a feeling. It emerges in relation to interpretation, to self-narrative, and to what the event appears to mean. A crisis of identity is never only a problem of self-definition. It also involves altered interpretation, emotional instability, and a disruption in meaning. A collapse of meaning does not remain philosophical for long. It changes emotion, thought, and self-organization alike.

This is why the metaphor of architecture is useful. In a building, a visible crack in one area may indicate stress distributed through the structure. In human experience, what appears as a difficulty in one domain may reflect tension across several at once. Rumination may not be only a thought problem. It may be thought under emotional strain in service of identity protection amid uncertainty of meaning. Emotional volatility may not be merely a matter of feeling too much. It may be the regulatory expression of deeper interpretive threat and identity instability. Emptiness may not be simple depression alone, but a broader reduction in meaningful integration across the whole architecture.

Once readers begin to see experience in this way, the framework becomes practical almost immediately. It changes what they notice. Instead of asking only, "Why do I feel this?" they may ask, "What interpretation is active here?" "What in my identity feels threatened?" "Why does this matter so much?" "What larger meaning is attached to this event?" A social injury, a professional failure, a family conflict, or a private fear begins to look different when viewed structurally. The person is no longer examining one symptom in isolation. They are learning to perceive the architecture through which the experience is being generated.

That does not mean they are stepping outside of human vulnerability. On the contrary, one of the values of structural understanding is that it often deepens compassion. When people understand how many forces are interacting inside a moment of distress, they are less likely to reduce themselves or others to simplistic judgments. A defensive reaction, an episode of collapse, a recurring avoidance, or a sudden crisis can be seen not only as behavior but as architecture under strain.

This chapter has been concerned with preparing the ground for that way of seeing. It has argued that human beings live within systems they rarely perceive directly, that fragmented psychology often leaves the whole person insufficiently understood, and that a structural perspective offers a more integrated way of making sense of human experience. The chapters that follow will examine each of the four domains in turn, beginning with the mind.

That sequence matters. Human beings first encounter the world through interpretation. They do not merely receive reality. They organize it. They construct patterns, assign significance, anticipate consequences, and build internal models of what is happening. The mind is therefore not only one domain among others. It is the interpretive engine through which the rest of the architecture is continuously engaged.

To understand the architecture of being human, it is necessary to begin there.

* * *

21

2

Mind: The Interpretive Engine

Human beings generally experience their minds as places where thoughts simply appear. Ideas arise, reactions form, memories surface, and interpretations follow events so quickly that they feel almost automatic. Most people therefore assume that the mind's role in experience is relatively straightforward: events occur in the world, the senses register them, and the mind processes what has already happened.

In everyday life this assumption seems perfectly reasonable. A person walks into a room and instantly recognizes the people present. They read a message and immediately understand its tone. They hear a remark during a conversation and quickly grasp what it means. In each of these cases the experience feels direct. Reality appears to present itself clearly, and the mind seems to recognize what is already there.

Yet this intuitive understanding turns out to be incomplete.

The mind does not simply record the world the way a camera records a scene. It actively organizes, interprets, and constructs experience. Before individuals become aware of what they are thinking or feeling, the mind has already performed a remarkable amount of work. It has filtered incoming information, compared it with past experiences, generated predictions about what is likely to occur, and assembled these elements into a coherent interpretation.

In other words, the mind functions less like a recording device and more

22

like an interpretive engine.

This interpretive activity is so rapid and continuous that it usually escapes notice. The human brain processes enormous quantities of information every second, yet conscious awareness receives only a small portion of the final result. What reaches awareness is not raw sensory data but an organized interpretation of that data. The mind has already decided what appears important, what appears threatening, what appears meaningful, and what can safely be ignored.

This process forms the first domain of Psychological Architecture.

Within the framework of Psychological Architecture, the mind is understood as the interpretive engine that organizes perception and assigns significance to experience. It is the system through which individuals make sense of what they encounter. The mind does not merely respond to events; it constructs the meaning of those events before emotional, identity-based, or existential responses emerge.

This interpretive function explains why human experience can vary so dramatically from one person to another. Two individuals may witness the same situation yet come away with entirely different impressions of what occurred. One person may interpret a conversation as supportive while another perceives it as critical. One may experience an unexpected change as an exciting opportunity, while another experiences it as a threat to stability.

The difference lies not only in personality or mood but in interpretation.

Interpretation determines what an event becomes within the psychological system. Before emotion responds and before identity organizes the event into personal narrative, the mind has already assigned meaning to what occurred.

This insight helps explain why the mind occupies such a central position within Psychological Architecture. Every other domain of experience depends on interpretation. Emotional responses arise in relation to the significance the mind assigns to events. Identity develops through repeated interpretations of personal experience across time. Meaning itself emerges through the narratives the mind constructs about life.

Understanding the mind as an interpretive engine therefore provides the foundation for understanding the rest of the architecture.

To see why this is true, it helps to begin with a simple observation about everyday experience. Human beings do not encounter the world as a stream of disconnected sensations. Instead, they experience events as meaningful patterns. Conversations feel friendly or hostile. Situations feel safe or dangerous. Opportunities feel promising or uncertain.

These meanings do not arise automatically from the events themselves. They arise through the interpretive work of the mind.

Consider how quickly interpretation occurs during social interaction. A brief pause in conversation may be interpreted as thoughtful reflection, awkward silence, or hidden disapproval. A short message may be interpreted as warm, neutral, or dismissive depending on tone and context. Even facial expressions, which seem straightforward, can carry multiple meanings depending on how they are interpreted.

In each of these situations the external signal is ambiguous. The mind resolves that ambiguity by selecting an interpretation that fits the available information and the individual's prior expectations.

The remarkable feature of this process is how seamlessly it occurs. Most of the time individuals are not aware that interpretation is happening at all. They experience the result of interpretation as if it were reality itself. The meaning of the event feels obvious and self-evident.

Only when interpretations conflict does the interpretive process become visible.

For example, two people might leave a meeting with very different impressions of what occurred. One believes the discussion was constructive and collaborative. The other feels that the conversation contained subtle criticism or hostility. Each individual may feel confident in their perception, even though the interpretations differ significantly.

Situations like this reveal an important fact about the mind: perception is inseparable from interpretation.

The brain does not simply receive information from the environment and pass it unchanged to consciousness. Instead, it actively organizes incoming information according to patterns learned from past experience. These patterns influence what individuals notice, how they interpret ambiguous events, and what conclusions they draw about what has happened.

Over time, these interpretive patterns become remarkably stable. The mind learns to anticipate familiar situations and quickly organizes perception according to those expectations. In many cases this stability is beneficial. It allows individuals to navigate complex environments efficiently without analyzing every detail from scratch.

However, the same interpretive stability that allows for efficient functioning can also create difficulties. When interpretive patterns become rigid, individuals may begin to see the world primarily through the lens of past experience. New situations are interpreted as repetitions of familiar ones, even when important differences exist.

A person who has repeatedly experienced criticism may begin to anticipate criticism in new environments. Someone who has learned to expect rejection may interpret neutral signals as signs of disapproval. Another who has experienced repeated success may approach unfamiliar challenges with confidence that they will ultimately succeed.

These tendencies do not represent flaws in the mind. They are natural consequences of an interpretive system designed to learn from experience. The brain constantly searches for patterns because recognizing patterns allows individuals to predict what might happen next.

Prediction is one of the mind's most powerful abilities. By anticipating likely outcomes, individuals can prepare for danger, seize opportunities, and coordinate their actions with others. The interpretive engine is therefore not only concerned with understanding the present but also with anticipating the future.

Yet prediction also increases the influence of past experience on present perception. The more the mind relies on established patterns, the more likely it is to interpret new situations through familiar narratives.

Within Psychological Architecture, this process is central to understanding how the psychological system organizes itself over time. Interpretations accumulate. Patterns of expectation form. Emotional responses become associated with particular meanings. Identity begins to incorporate these recurring interpretations into a narrative about who the person is and what the world is like.

Eventually, the individual may begin to experience these patterns as simple facts about reality rather than as interpretations that could potentially change.

Understanding the mind as an interpretive engine therefore invites a different way of examining psychological experience. Instead of asking only what someone feels or what happened in a particular situation, it becomes possible to ask how the mind interpreted the event in the first place.

This shift in perspective opens the door to a deeper understanding of human experience.

When interpretation becomes visible, patterns that once seemed mysterious begin to make sense. Emotional reactions reveal their connection to perceived meaning. Identity tensions reveal their roots in recurring interpretations of experience. Even questions about purpose and direction begin to appear differently when the interpretive system organizing those questions becomes clearer.

For this reason, the study of Psychological Architecture begins with the mind.

The interpretive engine is the gateway through which experience enters the psychological system. Everything that follows—emotion, identity, and meaning—emerges in response to the interpretations the mind constructs.

In the sections that follow, we will examine how the mind performs this interpretive work in greater detail. By understanding how perception becomes interpretation and how interpretation shapes emotional and behavioral responses, the deeper structure of psychological experience begins to come into view.

The architecture of being human begins with the way the mind makes sense of the world.

Interpretation alone, however, does not determine how individuals respond to experience. Once meaning has been assigned to an event, another system becomes active. The emotional system translates interpretation into urgency, motivation, and behavioral readiness. What the mind identifies as significant, the emotional system regulates through patterns of feeling and response. For this reason, understanding the architecture of human experience requires examining not only how events are interpreted but also how emotional signals organize the individual's reaction to those interpretations.

The Illusion of Direct Perception

Human beings experience the world as though they are encountering it directly. A person opens their eyes, looks around a room, and feels certain they are seeing what is there. They hear a sentence spoken in conversation and believe they have grasped its meaning immediately. They remember an event from the past and feel confident that the memory reflects what actually happened. In each of these cases the experience feels immediate and transparent. Reality seems to present itself clearly, and the mind seems to recognize it without difficulty.

Yet this sense of direct perception is largely an illusion.

What individuals experience as perception is the result of a complex interpretive process that occurs largely outside conscious awareness. The brain does not simply receive a complete picture of the external world. Instead, it receives fragments of sensory information—patterns of light entering the eyes, vibrations reaching the ears, pressure and temperature signals from the body. These signals are incomplete and often ambiguous. The mind must organize them into patterns that feel coherent and meaningful.

In other words, perception is constructed.

The brain continuously assembles sensory information into a working model of the world. It decides what elements of the environment deserve attention, what can be ignored, and how separate signals fit together into recognizable objects or events. Without this organizing process, the sensory world would appear chaotic and overwhelming.

Consider how quickly a person can recognize a familiar face in a crowd. The brain does not examine every feature one by one and then slowly arrive at a conclusion. Instead, it detects patterns that match previously stored memories. Recognition occurs almost instantly because the mind has learned the structure of faces through repeated experience.

This ability to recognize patterns is essential for survival. It allows individuals to identify threats quickly, coordinate social interaction, and navigate complex environments without conscious deliberation. However, pattern recognition also introduces interpretation into perception itself.

The brain is constantly comparing incoming sensory signals with patterns learned from the past. When the new information resembles a familiar pattern, the mind quickly interprets the situation as an instance of that pattern. This process happens so rapidly that individuals experience the interpretation as though it were simply part of perception.

For example, a person walking through a quiet neighborhood at night might suddenly notice a shadow moving in the distance. Within seconds the mind interprets the movement as either harmless or potentially threatening. If the shadow resembles the movement of a person approaching, the brain may generate a sense of alertness or concern. If the movement resembles an animal or blowing branches, the reaction may be minimal.

The key point is that the emotional response follows the interpretation. The shadow itself does not carry inherent meaning. Its significance emerges through the mind's interpretation of what it represents.

This relationship between perception and interpretation becomes especially visible in social situations. Human communication is filled with signals that require interpretation—tone of voice, facial expressions, pauses in speech, body posture, and subtle changes in language. None of these signals has a single fixed meaning. Instead, the mind must organize them into an interpretation of what another person intends.

A brief pause during conversation, for instance, might be interpreted as thoughtful reflection, hesitation, disagreement, or emotional discomfort. The mind selects the interpretation that seems most plausible given the context and prior expectations.

Because this interpretive process operates so quickly, individuals often believe they have directly perceived another person's intention. They may say, "I could tell she was upset," or "I knew he was criticizing me." Yet what they experienced was not direct access to another person's mind but an interpretation based on observable signals.

This interpretive nature of perception explains why misunderstandings are so common in human interaction. Two people may observe the same behavior and interpret it differently because their prior experiences, expectations, and emotional sensitivities differ.

For instance, imagine a situation in which a colleague offers a brief comment about a project during a meeting. One person might interpret the comment as constructive feedback, while another hears it as criticism. Each individual experiences their interpretation as obvious because it aligns with their existing expectations.

Such differences illustrate an important feature of the psychological system: perception is never completely neutral. It is shaped by the interpretive patterns the mind has developed through past experience.

Memory plays a crucial role in this process. The brain continuously compares present events with stored memories in order to determine what the current situation resembles. If a present event resembles a past experience that carried strong emotional significance, the mind may interpret the situation through that prior experience.

This is one reason certain environments can evoke powerful reactions even when nothing overtly threatening is occurring. A person who has experienced humiliation in a classroom may feel anxious returning to similar settings years later. Someone who has experienced rejection in relationships may interpret ambiguous signals from others as signs of disapproval.

In each case, perception is shaped by interpretive patterns formed through memory.

This does not mean the individual is consciously recalling the past event. The interpretive engine operates largely outside awareness. The person simply experiences the present situation as uncomfortable or threatening without immediately recognizing the interpretive pattern that produced the reaction.

Understanding the illusion of direct perception is therefore an essential step in understanding Psychological Architecture. It reveals that the mind is not a passive observer but an active participant in shaping experience.

Once this becomes clear, many aspects of psychological life begin to look different.

Emotional reactions become easier to understand when they are traced back to interpretation. Conflicts between individuals appear less mysterious when it becomes clear that each person is operating within a different interpretive framework. Even personal struggles such as anxiety, resentment, or self-doubt often reflect interpretive patterns that have become deeply embedded in the mind's expectations.

Recognizing the interpretive nature of perception does not eliminate the complexity of human experience. On the contrary, it reveals how deeply interpretation shapes the way individuals move through the world.

Events themselves may be shared, but the experience of those events is always filtered through the interpretive engine of the mind.

The next step is to examine how this interpretive engine constructs experience in more detail. By understanding the mechanisms through which the mind organizes perception—attention, pattern recognition, completion, and prediction—it becomes possible to see how interpretation develops and how it influences the rest of the psychological system.

Only then can we fully appreciate the central role the mind plays within the architecture of being human.

How the Mind Constructs Experience

Once the illusion of direct perception is set aside, a deeper question naturally emerges. If human beings do not simply perceive reality as it is, how exactly does the mind construct the experience that feels so immediate and convincing?

The answer lies in a set of processes through which the brain organizes sensory input into a coherent interpretation of the world. These processes operate continuously and largely outside conscious awareness. By the time individuals become aware of what they are thinking or feeling, the interpretive engine of the mind has already completed much of its work.

At the most basic level, the construction of experience begins with attention.

The sensory environment surrounding any individual at a given moment contains far more information than the brain could possibly process simultaneously. A crowded street contains thousands of visual details, overlapping conversations, movement in multiple directions, changing light patterns, and countless potential points of focus. If the brain attempted to process all of this information equally, the result would be overwhelming.

Attention acts as a filtering system. It selects certain aspects of the environment for detailed processing while allowing others to fade into the background. What receives attention becomes psychologically significant. What is ignored often disappears from conscious awareness entirely.

This filtering process is guided by a combination of goals, expectations, emotional relevance, and prior experience. A parent will immediately notice the sound of their child crying even in a noisy room. A driver scanning traffic will instinctively focus on potential hazards. A person who is anxious about evaluation may become acutely aware of subtle shifts in another person's tone or expression.

Through attention, the mind determines which elements of the environment will become part of the individual's psychological experience.

Yet attention alone does not produce meaning. The brain must also organize the information it receives.

This is where pattern recognition becomes essential.

Human beings are extraordinarily sensitive to patterns because recognizing patterns allows the brain to interpret complex situations quickly. When the mind encounters a familiar arrangement of signals—such as the configuration of a human face or the tone of a familiar voice—it can immediately identify what it represents.

Pattern recognition allows the brain to operate efficiently. Instead of analyzing every detail of a situation from scratch, the mind compares incoming information with previously learned structures. If the new information resembles an existing pattern, interpretation occurs almost instantly.

For example, when a person sees someone frowning with crossed arms and a tense posture, they may quickly interpret the expression as frustration or disagreement. They do not need to consciously analyze each feature of the scene. The mind recognizes the pattern and supplies the likely meaning.

This ability to detect patterns is one of the most powerful features of the human mind. It allows individuals to navigate social environments, anticipate danger, and coordinate behavior with remarkable speed.

However, pattern recognition also carries a potential cost. Once the mind has learned certain patterns, it may begin to apply them automatically even when the situation is only partially similar to past experience.

Imagine someone who has experienced repeated criticism from authority figures earlier in life. When they later receive feedback from a supervisor, the mind may quickly recognize a familiar pattern and interpret the feedback as criticism—even if the supervisor intended the comment to be supportive.

The interpretive engine is attempting to use past patterns to understand present events.

This dynamic illustrates why interpretation can sometimes feel automatic. The mind has learned to organize experience according to patterns that previously helped make sense of the world. When similar signals appear again, the brain applies those patterns rapidly.

A third process involved in constructing experience is completion.

Human perception rarely receives perfect information. Conversations are ambiguous, expressions are mixed, memories are incomplete, and circumstances change quickly. Rather than leaving these uncertainties unresolved, the brain fills in missing information to produce a coherent interpretation.

This tendency is visible in many aspects of daily life. A person might hear part of a sentence in a noisy room yet still understand the intended message because the brain fills in the missing words. Someone might remember the general feeling of a past event while unknowingly reconstructing many of the details.

Completion allows the mind to maintain continuity in experience even when information is incomplete.

Yet the same process can also contribute to misunderstanding. When the brain fills in gaps with assumptions that do not accurately reflect the situation, interpretation can drift away from what actually occurred.

A brief pause in conversation might be interpreted as disapproval rather than reflection. A delayed response to a message might be interpreted as rejection rather than distraction. In each case the mind completes the experience with an interpretation that feels coherent but may not be correct.

The final major process through which the mind constructs experience is prediction.

The brain is not only interpreting the present moment; it is constantly anticipating what will happen next. Based on past experience, the mind generates expectations about likely outcomes and prepares the body and attention accordingly.

Prediction allows individuals to move through the world efficiently. A person approaching a familiar intersection expects traffic to follow certain patterns. A speaker addressing an audience anticipates how listeners might respond. A friend in conversation predicts how the other person might finish a sentence.

This predictive capacity allows the brain to act quickly and confidently in complex environments.

But prediction also shapes perception itself.

When the mind strongly expects a particular outcome, it may interpret ambiguous signals as confirmation of that expectation. Someone who anticipates conflict may interpret neutral remarks as hostile. Someone who expects support may interpret the same remarks as constructive.

In this way, prediction reinforces interpretive patterns over time. The mind becomes increasingly confident in the narratives it has constructed about how the world works.

Attention, pattern recognition, completion, and prediction work together continuously to construct the experience individuals perceive as reality.

These processes are not flaws in the mind. They are essential features of how the brain functions. Without them, human beings would struggle to interpret the overwhelming complexity of the environment around them.

Yet these same processes also reveal why interpretation plays such a central role in Psychological Architecture.

Because experience is constructed through interpretation, the mind becomes the gateway through which events enter the psychological system. The meaning assigned to an event determines how the emotional system will respond, how the experience will be integrated into identity, and how it will influence the broader framework of meaning through which life is understood.

In this sense, interpretation does not merely describe events after they occur. It actively shapes what those events become within the psychological architecture of the individual.

The next section of this chapter explores how predictive interpretation influences emotional activation and how repeated interpretive patterns can gradually shape the structure of psychological life.

Prediction, Pattern, and the Human Brain

One of the most powerful characteristics of the human mind is its ability to anticipate what will happen next. The brain does not simply wait for events to unfold and then respond. Instead, it constantly generates expectations about the future based on patterns learned from past experience. These expectations influence what individuals notice, how they interpret events, and how they prepare to respond.

In recent decades, neuroscientists have increasingly described the brain as a predictive system. Rather than operating as a passive receiver of information, the brain continuously forecasts incoming signals and compares those predictions with what actually occurs. When new sensory information matches what the brain predicted, the mind experiences the situation as familiar and coherent. When the information contradicts expectations, the brain must revise its interpretation or update its predictive model.

This predictive process allows human beings to navigate the world efficiently. Without prediction, every moment would require careful analysis from the beginning. Even simple activities would become cognitively overwhelming. Walking through a crowded room, holding a conversation, or driving a car would require conscious attention to every detail of movement and sound.

Prediction allows the mind to operate with remarkable speed. When individuals enter familiar environments, they are not starting from zero. Their brains already carry models of how those environments typically behave. These models allow them to anticipate what will happen next.

A person entering their workplace in the morning already expects the layout of the building to remain stable. They anticipate where doors and hallways are located, how colleagues typically greet one another, and what tasks are likely to demand attention. Because these expectations are already in place, the mind can quickly detect anything unusual.

Prediction is therefore closely linked to pattern recognition. The mind stores patterns from past experience and uses those patterns to anticipate future events. When the brain recognizes a pattern that resembles something encountered before, it predicts how the situation is likely to unfold.

This capacity for prediction is one of the reasons human beings can move fluidly through complex social environments. In conversation, individuals often anticipate the direction of another person's sentence before it is finished. They recognize subtle shifts in tone or posture that signal emotional changes. They respond to questions and expressions almost instantly because their brains are constantly generating predictions about what those signals mean.

However, prediction also means that perception is never entirely neutral.

The mind does not simply observe the present moment. It interprets the present through expectations formed in the past. These expectations guide attention and shape the meaning assigned to events.

When predictive patterns are flexible, this process helps individuals adapt to new situations quickly. The mind adjusts its expectations as new information becomes available. Patterns evolve as experience accumulates.

But when predictive patterns become rigid, interpretation may begin to distort perception.

Imagine someone who has repeatedly experienced criticism from authority figures earlier in life. Over time, the brain may develop a predictive model in which authority figures are expected to be critical or dismissive. When the individual later interacts with supervisors, teachers, or other authority figures, the mind may anticipate criticism even when the situation is neutral.

Because the mind is predicting criticism, it begins to search for signals that confirm the expectation. A brief pause in conversation may be interpreted as disapproval. A suggestion for improvement may be interpreted as an attack. Even neutral expressions may appear negative when filtered through the predictive pattern.

In this way, prediction can subtly shape what the individual experiences as reality.

This process does not occur because the person is intentionally misinterpreting events. The predictive system is attempting to protect the individual by preparing them for familiar outcomes. The brain relies on past experience because past experience often provides useful guidance.

Yet the same process can lead to interpretive loops.

When the mind repeatedly predicts the same outcome, it becomes more sensitive to signals that confirm the prediction. Attention narrows to information that fits the pattern. Evidence that contradicts the pattern receives less attention or is interpreted in ways that preserve the existing expectation.

Over time the interpretive system can become increasingly confident in its predictive narrative.

For example, a person who repeatedly anticipates rejection may begin to interpret neutral social signals as signs of disinterest or disapproval. Because these interpretations trigger anxiety or withdrawal, the individual may behave in ways that unintentionally create distance in relationships. The resulting distance then appears to confirm the original expectation of rejection.

The predictive system has reinforced its own interpretation.

These loops illustrate how the interpretive engine can gradually shape the architecture of psychological experience. Predictive patterns influence perception, perception influences emotional response, and emotional response influences future interpretation.

The process becomes self-organizing.

Another example can be seen in professional environments. An individual who has experienced repeated success may develop a predictive model in which challenges are interpreted as opportunities for growth. When difficulties arise, the mind anticipates eventual success and organizes attention around strategies for solving the problem. The emotional response may include determination or curiosity rather than fear.

Here the predictive pattern supports resilience rather than distortion.

The difference between these outcomes lies not in whether prediction occurs but in how flexible the predictive system remains. When the mind can update its expectations in response to new information, interpretation remains adaptive. When predictive models become rigid, interpretation may become distorted.

Understanding this dynamic is essential for understanding the role of the mind within Psychological Architecture.

The interpretive engine does more than assign meaning to isolated events. It generates expectations about how the world works. These expectations influence how individuals perceive themselves, how they interpret others, and how they approach future situations.

Because prediction shapes interpretation, it indirectly shapes emotional experience as well. When the mind anticipates threat, the emotional system prepares for danger. When the mind anticipates opportunity, the emotional system mobilizes motivation.

Interpretation and emotion therefore operate in constant interaction.

The next domain of Psychological Architecture examines the emotional system itself. Emotion functions as the regulatory system of psychological life, signaling what matters and directing attention toward experiences that carry significance.

* * *

3

Emotion: The Regulatory System

Emotion occupies a central position in human experience. It shapes attention, directs behavior, influences memory, and signals what matters within the stream of life events. Most people are intimately familiar with emotional experience. They know what it feels like to become anxious before a difficult conversation, to feel anger in response to perceived injustice, to experience relief when a threat disappears, or to feel warmth and connection in the presence of someone they trust.

Yet despite this familiarity, emotion is often misunderstood.

Many individuals experience emotion primarily as something that happens to them. Emotions appear suddenly, sometimes with surprising intensity, and can seem difficult to control. A person may feel calm one moment and agitated the next. A comment from another person may trigger embarrassment or resentment almost instantly. A memory may evoke grief years after an event has occurred.

Because emotional responses can feel so immediate, it is easy to assume that emotions are simply reactions to external circumstances. Something happens, and emotion follows. When events are pleasant, positive emotions arise. When events are threatening or painful, negative emotions appear.

This description captures part of the truth, but it overlooks a deeper function of emotion within the psychological system.

Emotion does not exist merely as a reaction to experience. It functions as a regulatory system that helps organize how individuals respond to the world around them. Emotional signals direct attention toward events that carry significance, mobilize the body for action, and help determine how experiences will be integrated into memory and identity.

Within Psychological Architecture, emotion represents the second major domain of human experience. If the mind serves as the interpretive engine that assigns meaning to events, emotion functions as the regulatory system that responds to that meaning. The emotional system translates interpretation into motivation, urgency, and behavioral readiness.

Understanding this relationship between interpretation and emotion is essential. Emotional responses rarely arise in isolation. They emerge in response to the significance the mind assigns to events. When the mind interprets a situation as threatening, the emotional system activates fear or anxiety. When the mind interprets an event as unjust or violating personal boundaries, anger may arise. When interpretation frames an experience as meaningful or fulfilling, emotions such as joy, gratitude, or pride may follow.

Emotion therefore does not merely accompany experience. It regulates the organism's response to interpreted reality.

This regulatory function explains why emotions often feel powerful. Emotional signals evolved to direct attention toward what matters for survival, safety, belonging, and social coordination. When an event carries potential importance, the emotional system amplifies its significance by mobilizing attention and energy.

Fear prepares the body to detect and respond to danger. Anger mobilizes energy to confront perceived violations. Sadness slows activity and encourages reflection or social support after loss. Joy signals that circumstances support growth, connection, or fulfillment.

Each emotional state carries information about how the individual might respond to a situation.

From this perspective, emotion can be understood less as a disturbance of rational thought and more as an essential component of adaptive functioning. Emotional signals help prioritize attention in a world filled with competing demands. They guide decision-making when time is limited and uncertainty is high. They allow individuals to respond quickly to changes in their environment.

Yet emotional responses are not purely biological reflexes. Just as interpretation shapes perception, interpretation also shapes emotion.

A single event can evoke very different emotional reactions depending on how it is interpreted. A sudden job change might be experienced as exciting opportunity by one person and as destabilizing threat by another. A public performance may evoke exhilaration in someone who interprets the event as a chance for expression, while the same situation produces intense anxiety in someone who interprets it as a potential source of embarrassment.

The emotional system is responding not simply to the event itself but to the meaning assigned to the event.

This relationship between interpretation and emotion reveals why emotional experiences can sometimes feel confusing. Individuals may recognize that their emotional reaction seems disproportionate to the situation, yet still find it difficult to change the feeling. The emotional response follows the interpretation generated by the mind, and that interpretation may operate outside immediate awareness.

For example, a brief comment from a colleague might trigger strong irritation. On the surface the reaction may appear excessive. Yet if the comment activates an interpretation related to respect, competence, or status, the emotional system may respond with anger or defensiveness. The intensity of the reaction reflects the significance assigned to the event within the interpretive framework of the mind.

This dynamic illustrates the close relationship between the first two domains of Psychological Architecture. The mind interprets experience, and emotion regulates response to that interpretation.

Emotion also performs another important function within the psychological system: it helps determine what experiences become memorable.

Events associated with strong emotional activation tend to be remembered more vividly than emotionally neutral experiences. A person may forget the details of an ordinary afternoon yet recall with remarkable clarity a moment of embarrassment, triumph, or loss. Emotional intensity signals that an event carries significance, encouraging the brain to store the experience for future reference.

This process plays an important role in learning. By remembering emotionally significant experiences, individuals can adjust their behavior in the future. A painful mistake may encourage caution in similar circumstances. A rewarding success may reinforce behaviors that produced positive outcomes.

Over time, these emotionally marked memories contribute to the formation of identity. Repeated experiences of encouragement may support a narrative of competence and possibility. Repeated experiences of rejection may contribute to narratives of vulnerability or exclusion. Emotional patterns gradually become woven into the story individuals tell themselves about who they are.

In this way, the regulatory function of emotion extends beyond immediate reaction. Emotional signals help shape the long-term development of identity and meaning.

Yet the same mechanisms that make emotion adaptive can also produce difficulty when the regulatory system becomes strained.

If emotional signals become too intense or too frequent, they can overwhelm attention and narrow perception. Anxiety may cause the mind to focus almost exclusively on potential threats. Anger may limit the ability to consider alternative interpretations of a situation. Shame may lead individuals to withdraw from experiences that could challenge negative self-beliefs.

These patterns do not arise because emotion is inherently problematic. They arise when the regulatory system becomes locked into particular patterns of activation.

Understanding emotion as a regulatory system rather than merely a set of feelings provides a more nuanced view of psychological life. Emotional states are not simply disturbances that interfere with rational thinking. They are signals that organize attention, motivation, and behavior in response to interpreted events.

This understanding also helps explain why emotional experiences are deeply connected to other domains of Psychological Architecture.

Interpretation influences which emotions arise. Emotional signals influence what individuals attend to and remember. Those memories contribute to identity narratives about who a person is and how the world works. Identity, in turn, shapes future interpretations and emotional responses.

Emotion therefore occupies a pivotal position within the architecture of human experience.

To understand psychological stability and instability, it is necessary to understand how the emotional system regulates attention, motivation, and behavior in response to interpreted reality.

The Signaling Function of Emotion

Emotion serves as one of the most efficient signaling systems within human psychology. Long before individuals consciously analyze a situation, emotional signals begin directing attention toward what appears significant. A sudden feeling of unease may cause someone to notice subtle tension in a conversation. A surge of excitement may draw attention toward an opportunity that might otherwise have gone unnoticed. These signals function as internal alerts, helping the individual recognize what matters within a complex environment.

In this sense, emotion operates much like a priority system for the mind. The world contains far more information than any person can process at once. Conversations, responsibilities, relationships, physical surroundings, and internal thoughts compete for attention at every moment. Emotion helps determine which of these elements will become psychologically important.

When the emotional system detects something relevant to safety, belonging, or personal goals, it amplifies attention toward that element. Fear narrows attention to possible threats. Curiosity expands attention toward unfamiliar but potentially valuable information. Joy broadens perception and encourages engagement with the environment. Sadness slows activity and directs attention toward reflection or support from others.

These signals often appear automatic because they operate rapidly. The emotional system evolved to mobilize responses quickly, particularly in situations involving danger or opportunity. Waiting for slow analytical reasoning in such circumstances could prove costly. Emotion therefore functions as an early-warning system that alerts the organism to what requires immediate attention.

Consider how quickly emotional signals appear in everyday situations. A driver may feel a sudden surge of alarm before consciously recognizing that another vehicle has drifted into their lane. A parent may sense discomfort before realizing that something in a child's behavior has changed. A professional may feel excitement when hearing about a potential opportunity even before evaluating the details.

In each case, the emotional signal precedes deliberate reasoning. The body and mind respond to perceived significance before the individual has fully articulated what is happening.

This signaling function explains why emotional experiences often feel compelling. Emotional states influence perception, motivation, and action simultaneously. Fear prepares the body to move quickly, heightens awareness of danger, and discourages unnecessary risk. Anger mobilizes energy for confrontation when boundaries appear violated. Joy encourages exploration and social connection when circumstances appear favorable.

Emotion therefore acts as a bridge between perception and behavior.

Importantly, emotional signals do not simply reflect external events. They reflect the meaning those events carry within the individual's psychological system. When a situation is interpreted as threatening, the emotional system signals danger. When an event is interpreted as supportive or rewarding, emotion signals safety or opportunity.

Because interpretation shapes emotional signaling, individuals can experience different emotional reactions to the same situation. One person may interpret a challenging task as a chance for growth and feel energized. Another may interpret the same task as a potential failure and feel anxious or discouraged. The emotional signals differ because the interpretive meanings differ.

This interaction between interpretation and emotion highlights the complexity of psychological experience. Emotional responses cannot be fully understood without considering how events are interpreted. At the same time, interpretation alone does not capture the urgency and motivational power that emotional signals provide.

Emotion brings interpretation to life.

Without emotional signaling, interpretations would remain abstract cognitive events. A person might recognize that a situation carries potential importance but feel no motivation to act. Emotional activation transforms interpretation into felt significance. It signals that something requires attention, preparation, or response.

The signaling function of emotion also plays a crucial role in social interaction. Humans are highly sensitive to emotional cues in others. Facial expressions, tone of voice, posture, and subtle behavioral signals communicate emotional states that influence how interactions unfold.

A slight shift in expression can signal approval or disappointment. A warm tone of voice can signal welcome and trust. A tense posture may indicate discomfort or defensiveness. Individuals often respond to these signals automatically, adjusting their behavior without consciously analyzing the cues.

Through this process, emotional signaling helps coordinate social relationships. It allows individuals to respond to one another's needs, intentions, and concerns. Without emotional cues, human communication would become far more difficult.

However, the same sensitivity that enables social coordination can also create misunderstanding. Because emotional signals are interpreted through the mind's predictive patterns, individuals may sometimes misread what others are feeling or intending. A neutral expression may be interpreted as disapproval. A brief pause in conversation may be interpreted as rejection. In such cases the interpretive engine shapes how emotional signals are perceived.

The interaction between emotional signaling and interpretation therefore forms a continuous loop. Interpretation influences which emotional signals arise, and emotional signals influence what interpretations feel convincing.

Over time, these loops contribute to the development of stable emotional patterns. Individuals may become accustomed to interpreting situations in ways that repeatedly trigger particular emotional responses. Someone who frequently interprets uncertainty as danger may experience chronic anxiety. Someone who interprets challenges as opportunities may experience excitement and determination in similar situations.

These patterns become part of the individual's psychological landscape. Emotional responses begin to feel predictable and characteristic of the person's personality or temperament.

Yet emotional patterns are not fixed traits. They are dynamic responses within a regulatory system that interacts continuously with interpretation, identity, and meaning. Changes in how events are interpreted can alter emotional signaling. Changes in identity or purpose can transform how situations are experienced emotionally.

Understanding emotion as a signaling system therefore reveals its flexibility as well as its power. Emotional states communicate what matters, but they do so within the interpretive frameworks the mind provides.

Within Psychological Architecture, this signaling function represents one of the central ways the emotional system regulates experience. By directing attention and motivation toward significant events, emotion helps organize how individuals move through the world.

Emotional signals guide what individuals notice, what they remember, and how they respond. Through these signals, the regulatory system of emotion shapes the flow of psychological life from moment to moment.

Emotional Regulation and Human Behavior

Emotion does not only signal what matters. It also regulates how individuals respond once significance has been detected. When an emotional state emerges, it does more than produce a feeling. It prepares the body and mind for action. It shifts attention, adjusts physiological readiness, and influences the range of behaviors that feel available in a given moment.

This regulatory role is one of the reasons emotion is so central to human behavior. People often assume that decisions arise primarily from deliberate reasoning. Yet in practice, emotional states frequently guide what individuals do long before they consciously analyze a situation.

When fear arises, the body prepares for rapid movement and heightened vigilance. Heart rate increases, attention narrows toward possible threats, and the mind begins searching for ways to escape or avoid danger. These changes occur quickly because fear evolved to mobilize protective responses. The emotional system is preparing the organism to survive.

Anger produces a different pattern of regulation. Instead of withdrawal, anger often mobilizes energy for confrontation. The body becomes activated, attention focuses on perceived violations, and the individual may feel an urge to defend boundaries or challenge a threat. This response can be adaptive when genuine injustices occur, but it can also become problematic if the interpretive system repeatedly signals violation in situations that do not require confrontation.

Other emotions regulate behavior in subtler ways. Sadness tends to slow activity and encourage withdrawal from demanding tasks. This slowing allows time for reflection, recovery, and social support after loss or disappointment. Joy and enthusiasm, in contrast, broaden behavioral possibilities. Individuals experiencing these states are more likely to explore new opportunities, engage socially, and pursue goals with energy.

Each emotional state therefore carries a regulatory pattern that influences how behavior unfolds.

These patterns often operate outside conscious awareness. A person experiencing anxiety may find themselves repeatedly checking for potential problems without deliberately deciding to do so. Someone feeling confident and energized may speak more freely and take initiative without carefully planning each step.

Emotion is guiding behavior by shaping which actions feel natural or compelling in the moment.

This regulatory influence also explains why emotional states can alter how individuals think. When anxiety dominates attention, the mind becomes preoccupied with potential risks and negative outcomes. When anger is active, interpretations may become sharper and more judgmental. When joy is present, individuals may perceive possibilities that previously felt inaccessible.

Emotion therefore regulates not only behavior but cognition as well.

From the perspective of Psychological Architecture, this regulatory function connects emotion directly with the interpretive engine of the mind. Interpretation generates meaning, and emotional regulation organizes how the individual responds to that meaning.

If the mind interprets a situation as threatening, emotional regulation prepares the organism to protect itself. If interpretation frames the same situation as an opportunity, emotional regulation mobilizes motivation and curiosity.

Because emotional regulation depends on interpretation, the same external circumstances can produce dramatically different behavioral responses across individuals.

Imagine two people invited to speak before a large audience. One person may interpret the event as an exciting chance to share ideas and connect with others. The emotional system responds with anticipation and energy. Their behavior reflects confidence and engagement.

Another person may interpret the same invitation as a situation in which embarrassment or failure is likely. The emotional system signals danger, producing anxiety and tension. Their behavior may include hesitation, avoidance, or intense self-monitoring.

The difference between these reactions lies not in the event itself but in the interpretive meaning assigned to it and the emotional regulation that follows.

Over time, patterns of emotional regulation can become deeply embedded within an individual's psychological system. Repeated experiences of anxiety may condition the mind to anticipate threat in many situations. Repeated experiences of encouragement and success may condition the emotional system to respond with confidence.

These patterns gradually influence how individuals approach life.

Someone whose emotional system frequently signals danger may become cautious and vigilant in unfamiliar situations. Someone whose emotional system often signals opportunity may approach new experiences with curiosity and initiative. Neither pattern is inherently fixed or permanent, but repeated activation strengthens the pathways through which emotional regulation operates.

Another important aspect of emotional regulation involves the body.

Emotional states are not purely mental experiences. They involve physiological changes that influence breathing, muscle tension, heart rate, and hormonal activity. These changes prepare the organism to act in ways consistent with the emotional signal.

Anxiety may produce tightness in the chest or stomach, reflecting the body's preparation for vigilance. Anger may create warmth and muscular tension, reflecting readiness for confrontation. Joy may produce relaxation and openness, reflecting a sense of safety.

These bodily shifts contribute to the intensity of emotional experience. Because emotion is embodied, individuals often feel emotional states before they can clearly articulate what those states mean.

The body therefore participates in emotional regulation alongside the mind.

Understanding this connection helps explain why emotional states can sometimes feel difficult to change through reasoning alone. If the body has already mobilized for a particular response, simply telling oneself that the situation is safe may not immediately reverse the physiological activation. Emotional regulation involves coordinated changes in interpretation, physiology, and behavior.

Yet emotional regulation also demonstrates the remarkable adaptability of the human psychological system. As individuals encounter new experiences, develop new interpretations, and form new patterns of response, emotional regulation can gradually shift.

Someone who once experienced intense anxiety in social situations may, through repeated positive experiences, begin to associate those situations with curiosity rather than threat. Someone who once reacted with anger to perceived criticism may learn to interpret feedback as an opportunity for growth.

These changes illustrate the dynamic nature of emotional regulation.

Emotion is not a static trait that determines behavior permanently. It is an active regulatory system that responds to interpretation, experience, and learning over time. Within Psychological Architecture, this regulatory system plays a crucial role in shaping how individuals move through the world, respond to challenges, and pursue meaningful goals.

When Emotional Regulation Becomes Unstable

Emotional regulation allows human beings to respond adaptively to the world around them. In most circumstances, emotional signals rise and fall in ways that correspond to changing conditions. A moment of fear passes once danger disappears. Frustration fades when a problem is resolved. Joy softens as attention shifts to other tasks. The emotional system is designed to adjust continuously, helping the individual remain responsive to the environment.

However, emotional regulation does not always operate smoothly. There are times when emotional states become unusually persistent, unusually intense, or unusually difficult to shift. In such situations the regulatory system may begin to function in ways that feel unstable.

This instability does not mean that emotion itself is defective. Rather, it reflects the complexity of the psychological architecture within which emotion operates. Emotional signals are shaped by interpretation, memory, bodily activation, and social experience. When patterns within these systems reinforce one another, emotional responses may become amplified or prolonged.

One way instability appears is through emotional amplification.

Amplification occurs when emotional signals escalate beyond the demands of the immediate situation. A small criticism may trigger intense anger. A minor uncertainty may produce overwhelming anxiety. A brief disappointment may lead to extended periods of discouragement. In these moments the emotional system responds not only to the present event but also to layers of prior interpretation and memory that the event has activated.

Because the emotional system is sensitive to significance, situations that touch on deeply held concerns can quickly activate powerful responses. If an individual has experienced repeated rejection in the past, even subtle signs of disapproval may carry heavy emotional weight. The emotional signal is responding to a perceived pattern rather than to the isolated moment itself.

Amplification therefore often reflects accumulated emotional history.

Another form of instability appears through emotional persistence.

Persistence occurs when an emotional state continues long after the circumstances that triggered it have changed. Someone who experienced embarrassment during a meeting may replay the event repeatedly for hours or days. Someone who felt anger during an argument may remain emotionally activated even after the conflict has ended.

This persistence often arises because the interpretive engine of the mind continues revisiting the event. Each time the situation is mentally replayed, the emotional system responds again as though the event were still occurring. The loop between interpretation and emotion sustains the regulatory state.

In these cases, emotion is not regulating response to the present moment. It is regulating response to an ongoing internal narrative.

Emotional instability may also appear through narrowing.

When the emotional system becomes strongly activated, attention often contracts around the signals associated with that emotion. Anxiety narrows attention toward potential threats. Anger narrows attention toward perceived violations. Sadness narrows attention toward themes of loss or disappointment.

This narrowing can make it difficult for individuals to perceive alternative interpretations of a situation. When anxiety dominates attention, neutral signals may be interpreted as signs of danger. When anger dominates attention, complex interactions may appear as simple conflicts between right and wrong.

Because emotional states influence what the mind notices, they can gradually reinforce their own perspective. The individual begins seeing the world through the lens of the dominant emotion.

Over time this narrowing may contribute to rigid emotional patterns. A person who frequently experiences anxiety may begin to interpret many situations as potentially threatening. Someone who frequently experiences anger may interpret ambiguous events as evidence of disrespect or injustice. The regulatory system becomes accustomed to activating the same emotional response across many contexts.

These patterns do not develop intentionally. They emerge gradually through repeated cycles of interpretation and emotional activation.

Another aspect of emotional instability involves the relationship between emotion and avoidance.

When emotional states become intensely uncomfortable, individuals often attempt to escape or suppress those feelings. Avoidance can take many forms. Someone may withdraw from situations that trigger anxiety, distract themselves from painful memories, or attempt to suppress emotional reactions entirely.

While avoidance can provide temporary relief, it often leaves the underlying interpretive patterns unchanged. Because the emotional system never has the opportunity to update its response to the situation, the same signals may arise again in future circumstances.

In this way, avoidance can unintentionally reinforce emotional instability.

The regulatory system becomes organized around preventing emotional discomfort rather than integrating emotional experience. Situations associated with strong emotion remain psychologically unresolved, and the emotional system remains sensitive to similar signals in the future.

Yet even when emotional instability appears, the regulatory system is still performing its fundamental function. It is signaling significance, directing attention, and preparing the organism to respond to perceived conditions. The difficulty arises when the interpretive patterns guiding those signals become overly rigid or misaligned with present circumstances.

Understanding this dynamic is essential for understanding emotional life within Psychological Architecture.

Emotion is not simply a collection of feelings that appear unpredictably. It is a regulatory system that organizes behavior, attention, and memory in response to interpreted meaning. When the interpretive engine repeatedly signals threat, violation, or loss, the emotional system responds accordingly.

Over time, these repeated signals can shape the broader structure of psychological experience. Emotional patterns begin influencing how individuals see themselves, how they interpret others, and how they approach the future.

At this point the architecture of identity begins to emerge. Emotional experiences accumulate into narratives about who a person is and how the world works. The next domain of Psychological Architecture explores how these narratives form and how identity organizes human experience over time.

Emotion, Memory, and the Shaping of Experience

Emotion does more than signal significance and regulate behavior in the present moment. It also plays a decisive role in determining what becomes part of an individual's psychological history. Experiences that carry strong emotional activation tend to leave deeper impressions in memory, while emotionally neutral moments often fade quickly from awareness.

This selective imprinting is not accidental. The human brain evolved to remember experiences that carry consequences for survival, safety, and social belonging. Emotion acts as a marker that tells the brain, in effect, "This matters. Remember this."

When individuals recall events from their lives, they rarely retrieve a perfectly neutral record of what occurred. Instead, they tend to remember moments that were emotionally charged. A painful embarrassment in childhood, the excitement of an early success, the warmth of a meaningful relationship, or the grief of a loss may remain vivid long after the surrounding details have faded.

Emotion functions as a kind of highlighting mechanism within the stream of experience. It selects certain moments for preservation while allowing others to pass quietly into the background of memory.

This process has profound consequences for how individuals come to understand their own lives.

Because emotionally intense experiences are more likely to be remembered, they often exert disproportionate influence on the stories people tell about themselves. A few moments of rejection may overshadow many ordinary interactions. A single triumph may shape a person's sense of capability for years. A painful failure may linger in memory long after other achievements have been forgotten.

The emotional system is not trying to create a balanced narrative. It is attempting to preserve experiences that appear significant.

Memory therefore becomes intertwined with emotional regulation. When an emotionally charged memory is recalled, the emotional system often activates again in response to the remembered event. A person remembering an argument may feel anger or embarrassment even if the conflict occurred years earlier. Someone recalling a joyful experience may feel warmth and gratitude as though the moment were happening again.

In this way, emotion allows past experiences to remain psychologically alive.

This capacity has clear advantages. By revisiting emotionally meaningful experiences, individuals can learn from the past and adjust their behavior in the future. A memory associated with danger may encourage caution in similar situations. A memory associated with success may inspire confidence when facing new challenges.

Yet emotional memory also shapes perception in more subtle ways.

Because emotionally charged experiences are remembered more vividly, they can begin to influence how new situations are interpreted. A person who remembers several painful social interactions may approach unfamiliar conversations with heightened vigilance. Someone who recalls repeated encouragement may approach new opportunities with optimism.

The interpretive engine of the mind uses emotionally marked memories as reference points when predicting what might happen next.

Over time, clusters of emotionally significant memories begin to form patterns. Individuals may come to see themselves as capable or incapable, accepted or excluded, resilient or fragile. These conclusions do not emerge from a careful statistical analysis of all life experiences. They emerge from the emotional weight carried by particular memories.

This dynamic helps explain why people sometimes hold strong beliefs about themselves even when those beliefs do not fully reflect their broader experience. A few emotionally intense events may carry enough influence to shape the narrative through which a person interprets the rest of their life.

Emotion therefore contributes not only to memory but to meaning.

When individuals recall their past, they rarely remember events as isolated moments. They organize experiences into stories that help explain who they are and how their lives have unfolded. Emotion provides the connective tissue for these stories. Moments associated with strong emotional signals become anchors around which personal narratives are constructed.

A person who vividly remembers moments of support and encouragement may construct a narrative of belonging and possibility. Someone whose most powerful memories involve criticism or rejection may construct a narrative centered on vulnerability or self-protection.

These narratives are not fixed or inevitable. They evolve as new experiences occur and as individuals reinterpret the past in light of present understanding. Yet the emotional intensity associated with particular memories often determines which experiences feel most central to the story of one's life.

Emotion, memory, and interpretation therefore form a tightly connected system.

Interpretation assigns meaning to events. Emotion signals the significance of that meaning. Memory preserves emotionally significant moments for future reference. Those memories then influence how new experiences are interpreted, which in turn shapes future emotional responses.

This recursive loop operates continuously throughout human life.

Consider how quickly this cycle can unfold in everyday situations. A person who once felt embarrassed while speaking in public may carry a vivid memory of that moment. When another opportunity to speak arises, the mind recalls the memory and predicts a similar outcome. The emotional system activates anxiety in response to the anticipated threat. The individual's attention narrows toward possible mistakes, and the experience becomes more difficult.

The emotional memory has influenced interpretation, which has influenced emotional regulation again.

The same mechanism can also reinforce confidence and growth. Someone who remembers successfully overcoming previous challenges may approach new difficulties with a sense of possibility. The mind predicts that effort will lead to progress, the emotional system responds with motivation, and the individual engages the challenge more fully.

In this case the emotional memory supports adaptive regulation.

These examples illustrate how emotion participates in shaping the broader architecture of experience. Emotional signals do not simply arise and disappear. They leave traces in memory that influence how individuals interpret the world in the future.

As these traces accumulate, they begin to influence how a person understands themselves.

Repeated emotional experiences gradually contribute to the formation of a stable sense of self. Individuals begin to organize their memories into narratives that explain their character, their relationships, and their place in the world. These narratives become part of the psychological structure through which life is interpreted.

Emotion therefore plays a foundational role not only in regulating immediate behavior but also in shaping the long-term structure of human experience.

Through its influence on memory, emotion helps determine which moments become meaningful landmarks in the landscape of a person's life.

Over time, repeated emotional experiences do more than regulate moment-to-moment behavior. They gradually become woven into the narrative structure through which individuals understand themselves. Patterns of emotional response influence how people interpret their past, how they anticipate the future, and how they evaluate their own capacities and vulnerabilities. In this way, emotional life becomes inseparable from the development of identity. To understand the architecture of human experience more fully, it is therefore necessary to examine how the self itself becomes organized across time.

* * *

56

4

Identity: The Organizing Narrative

Every human being carries a sense of who they are. It is rarely something people articulate in precise language, yet it quietly shapes how they move through the world. Individuals know what kinds of situations feel natural to them and which ones feel uncomfortable. They have assumptions about their abilities, their value, their role in relationships, and the kinds of futures that seem possible.

This sense of self is what we refer to as identity.

Identity is often discussed as though it were a collection of traits or labels. People describe themselves as confident or shy, independent or loyal, analytical or creative. They may identify with particular roles such as parent, teacher, artist, or leader. They may also describe themselves through social categories that signal belonging within larger groups.

While these descriptions capture certain aspects of identity, they do not fully explain how identity functions within the architecture of human experience.

Within Psychological Architecture, identity is best understood not simply as a set of characteristics but as an organizing narrative. It is the evolving story through which individuals interpret their past, understand their present, and imagine their future. This narrative does not exist only in words. It is embedded in memory, emotional patterns, expectations, and habitual interpretations.

Identity organizes experience by answering a series of implicit questions.
Who am I?
What kind of person am I becoming?
What should I expect from the world?
What does my life mean?

These questions are rarely considered directly in daily life, yet the answers shape perception, decision-making, and emotional responses. The story individuals hold about themselves becomes the framework through which events are interpreted.

Consider how differently a situation may be experienced depending on the identity narrative a person carries. Someone who sees themselves as capable and resilient may approach difficulty with determination. Challenges become tests of skill rather than threats to self-worth. Another person who holds a narrative of inadequacy may encounter the same difficulty and immediately interpret it as evidence of personal failure.

The external circumstances may be identical, but the identity narrative organizes how the experience is understood.

This organizing function makes identity one of the most powerful forces within psychological life. It influences what individuals notice, how they interpret events, and what possibilities they consider available to them. Identity provides continuity across time, allowing people to experience themselves as the same person from one moment to the next despite constant changes in circumstances.

Without such continuity, human experience would feel fragmented. Each event would stand alone without connection to the broader story of a person's life.

Identity provides the structure that links experiences together.

The formation of identity begins early in life, though it continues evolving across the lifespan. From childhood onward, individuals begin interpreting their experiences in ways that gradually shape their understanding of who they are. Feedback from caregivers, peers, teachers, and cultural environments contributes to this process. Moments of encouragement, criticism, belonging, and exclusion all become part of the developing narrative.

These experiences do not simply accumulate as isolated memories. They become woven into patterns that give the individual's life a sense of coherence.

A child repeatedly praised for creativity may begin to see themselves as imaginative or expressive. Another child frequently criticized for mistakes may begin to interpret new situations with caution, expecting evaluation or correction. These early interpretations begin forming narrative threads that extend into later stages of life.

Emotion plays a central role in determining which experiences become part of this narrative structure. As discussed in the previous chapter, emotionally intense experiences are more likely to be remembered and integrated into personal memory. These memories then influence how individuals interpret subsequent events.

A moment of encouragement may strengthen a sense of competence. A moment of humiliation may reinforce a sense of vulnerability. Over time, clusters of emotionally significant memories begin to form the backbone of identity.

This process does not require deliberate reflection. Most people do not consciously decide what their identity will be. Instead, identity emerges gradually from the interaction between interpretation, emotion, and memory.

The mind interprets events.

Emotion signals their significance.

Memory preserves those experiences.

Identity then organizes them into a story that explains who the individual is.

Once this narrative begins to take shape, it influences future interpretation. Individuals tend to interpret new experiences in ways that maintain coherence with their existing sense of self. Events that fit the narrative are easily integrated. Events that contradict it may be reinterpreted, minimized, or overlooked.

For example, a person who sees themselves as socially awkward may remember moments of embarrassment vividly while overlooking moments of successful interaction. Another person who views themselves as capable may treat temporary setbacks as exceptions rather than defining experiences.

Identity therefore functions as both organizer and filter.

It organizes the past into a coherent narrative and filters present experiences according to that narrative. This filtering process allows individuals to maintain a stable sense of self even when circumstances change.

Yet the stability provided by identity carries both advantages and limitations.

On the one hand, a coherent identity supports psychological resilience. When individuals understand themselves within a meaningful narrative, they can interpret difficulties as part of a larger story rather than as isolated failures. A person who sees themselves as persistent may view setbacks as temporary obstacles. Someone who identifies strongly with values of compassion may find meaning even in difficult circumstances.

Identity provides continuity and direction.

On the other hand, identity can also constrain perception. When a narrative becomes rigid, individuals may struggle to recognize possibilities that fall outside the story they hold about themselves. Someone who believes they are incapable of leadership may avoid opportunities to lead even when they possess the necessary skills. Someone who sees themselves as unworthy of connection may withdraw from relationships that could challenge that belief.

In these cases, identity does not simply describe experience. It shapes the range of experiences individuals consider possible.

Understanding identity as an organizing narrative helps illuminate how human lives acquire coherence across time. Experiences accumulate, memories form patterns, and emotional signals highlight moments of significance. Identity gathers these elements into a story that allows the individual to make sense of their life.

This story is never completely fixed. As individuals encounter new experiences and reinterpret the past, the narrative can evolve. Yet at any given moment, identity provides the interpretive framework through which life events are understood.

Within Psychological Architecture, identity represents the third domain of human experience. It organizes the patterns generated by the interpretive engine of the mind and the regulatory signals of emotion. Through identity, the events of life become part of a coherent psychological structure that guides perception, behavior, and meaning across time.

How Humans Become the Stories They Tell

Identity does not appear suddenly as a finished concept. It develops gradually as individuals attempt to make sense of their experiences over time. Human beings are natural meaning-makers. When events occur, people rarely experience them as isolated incidents. Instead, they instinctively connect those events to a broader understanding of who they are and how the world works.

This process unfolds through narrative.

Narrative is the mind's way of organizing experience across time. A narrative links past events to present circumstances and future expectations. It explains how things came to be the way they are and suggests where they might be heading next. Through narrative, individuals transform scattered memories into a coherent story.

Identity is the narrative individuals construct about themselves.

This story is rarely written down or consciously rehearsed. Instead, it exists as a quiet framework within which experiences are interpreted. People carry assumptions about their character, their abilities, their relationships, and the direction of their lives. These assumptions influence how they understand new events as they occur.

Consider how quickly individuals interpret everyday situations through the lens of identity. A student who sees themselves as capable may treat a poor grade as a temporary setback. The narrative of competence remains intact, and the student focuses on improvement. Another student who views themselves as inadequate may interpret the same grade as confirmation of a deeper belief about their limitations.

The event itself remains unchanged. What changes is the narrative through which it is understood.

Narratives develop because the human mind seeks coherence. Without some form of narrative structure, experiences would appear disconnected and confusing. Individuals would struggle to understand how the past relates to the present or how their actions influence future outcomes.

Narrative provides continuity.

It explains why earlier events occurred and how they shaped the person who exists today. When individuals recall their past, they rarely retrieve events in a purely chronological sequence. Instead, they organize memories into meaningful episodes that illustrate aspects of their identity. Certain moments become symbolic turning points in the story of a life.

A career choice may be remembered as a defining decision. A personal loss may become a moment that reshaped one's outlook. A relationship may represent a chapter of growth, conflict, or transformation.

These narrative markers help individuals make sense of the passage of time.

Emotion plays a decisive role in determining which events become part of the narrative. As discussed earlier, emotionally intense experiences tend to remain more vivid in memory. These experiences are therefore more likely to become central elements in the stories people tell about themselves.

Moments of embarrassment, pride, love, rejection, success, and failure often become narrative anchors. They are remembered not only for what happened but for what they seemed to reveal about the individual.

A person may remember the first time they spoke confidently in front of a group and interpret it as evidence of emerging capability. Another may remember a humiliating mistake and interpret it as evidence of personal inadequacy. Over time, these emotionally significant moments accumulate and form patterns.

Those patterns gradually become the storyline of identity.

Importantly, the narrative of identity is not simply a record of events. It is an interpretation of events. Individuals constantly reinterpret their experiences in ways that preserve coherence with their existing sense of self.

For example, someone who sees themselves as resilient may interpret past hardships as challenges that strengthened their character. Someone who sees themselves as unfortunate may interpret the same hardships as evidence that life is unfair or unkind. The narrative organizes the meaning of the events rather than merely recording them.

This interpretive flexibility allows identity to remain stable even as circumstances change. When new experiences occur, the narrative adapts by incorporating them into the existing storyline.

Yet this flexibility has limits.

When identity becomes strongly established, individuals may unconsciously filter new experiences in ways that preserve the existing narrative. Evidence that fits the story is easily accepted. Evidence that contradicts the story may be dismissed, minimized, or reinterpreted.

A person who believes they are socially awkward may overlook moments of successful connection. A person who believes they are competent may treat failures as unusual exceptions rather than meaningful signals.

In this way, identity can become self-reinforcing.

The narrative through which individuals interpret their lives begins influencing the kinds of experiences they notice, the risks they take, and the opportunities they pursue. Over time, behavior shaped by identity can produce outcomes that appear to confirm the narrative itself.

Someone who believes they are incapable of leadership may avoid leadership opportunities. Because they never test that assumption, the belief remains intact. Someone who believes they are capable of growth may continue seeking challenges, gradually accumulating experiences that support that identity.

Narrative and behavior therefore interact continuously.

Identity also influences relationships. The story individuals carry about themselves shapes how they interpret the intentions and reactions of others. Someone who believes they are valued may interpret neutral interactions as friendly or supportive. Someone who believes they are unwanted may interpret the same interactions as signs of rejection.

These interpretations influence how individuals behave toward others, which in turn shapes the responses they receive.

In this way, identity does not exist only within the individual. It becomes woven into patterns of social interaction.

Another important feature of identity narratives is their ability to simplify complexity. Human lives contain countless experiences, many of which contradict one another. Individuals may demonstrate courage in one moment and hesitation in another. They may show kindness in some relationships and impatience in others.

Identity narratives simplify this complexity by highlighting certain patterns and minimizing others. A person may emphasize experiences that support a particular self-concept while overlooking experiences that complicate that image.

This simplification helps maintain coherence, but it can also obscure the full range of a person's capabilities and possibilities.

Recognizing identity as a narrative structure allows individuals to see that the story they carry about themselves is not identical to the entirety of their experience. It is an interpretation of that experience organized around themes that feel psychologically meaningful.

Within Psychological Architecture, identity represents the domain in which interpretation, emotion, and memory converge into a coherent story about the self. The narrative that emerges from this convergence becomes the framework through which individuals understand who they are and what their lives represent.

Through this process, human beings quite literally become the stories they tell about themselves.

Memory, Coherence, and the Construction of Self

If identity is the story individuals carry about who they are, memory provides the raw material from which that story is constructed. Without memory, identity would have no continuity. Each moment of experience would exist in isolation, disconnected from what came before. Individuals would be unable to recognize themselves as the same person across time.

Memory allows the self to extend beyond the present moment.

Yet memory does not operate like a neutral recording device that stores events exactly as they occurred. Instead, memory is selective, interpretive, and reconstructive. The brain retains fragments of experience—images, emotions, sensations, and meanings—and later reassembles those fragments into recollections that feel coherent.

This reconstructive quality of memory plays a crucial role in shaping identity.

When individuals remember their past, they do not retrieve a complete archive of events. They retrieve experiences that appear relevant to the story they hold about themselves. Certain memories become central landmarks within the narrative of identity, while countless other moments fade into the background of psychological life.

Emotion, as discussed earlier, plays a decisive role in determining which memories remain vivid. Experiences associated with strong emotional activation tend to persist because they carry signals of significance. A moment of embarrassment during adolescence may remain clear decades later. A moment of encouragement from a mentor may become a defining memory that influences future aspirations.

These emotionally marked memories become anchors within the narrative of identity.

Yet memory does more than preserve the past. It organizes the past into patterns that appear meaningful in the present. Individuals tend to remember experiences in ways that reinforce the coherence of their identity narrative.

For example, someone who sees themselves as resilient may recall past difficulties as evidence of perseverance. They may remember the effort required to overcome obstacles and the satisfaction that followed. Another individual who views themselves as vulnerable may remember the same kinds of events as proof that life is unpredictable or unfair.

The memories themselves may involve similar circumstances, yet the meanings attached to them differ because the identity narrative differs.

This process reflects a powerful psychological need for coherence.

Human beings are uncomfortable with fragmented or contradictory self-understandings. When memories conflict with the existing narrative of identity, individuals often reinterpret those memories in ways that restore coherence. An embarrassing mistake may be reframed as a learning experience. A moment of kindness may be dismissed as unusual if it contradicts a deeply held belief about one's character.

Through this process, memory and identity continuously shape one another.

Identity influences which memories are emphasized and how they are interpreted. Memory, in turn, provides the evidence that sustains the narrative of identity. The story of the self becomes a dynamic structure maintained through the ongoing interpretation of remembered experiences.

This relationship between memory and identity can be seen clearly when individuals revisit important life events. Over time, people often reinterpret the meaning of past experiences as their perspective changes.

A painful setback that once felt humiliating may later appear as a turning point that redirected a person toward a more meaningful path. A relationship that once seemed central to one's identity may later be understood as one chapter within a much larger story. These reinterpretations illustrate how memory remains flexible even as identity seeks coherence.

Memory therefore serves two complementary functions within Psychological Architecture.

First, it preserves experiences that carry emotional and personal significance. Second, it organizes those experiences into patterns that help individuals understand who they are.

Together, these functions create the sense of continuity that allows individuals to experience themselves as the same person across time. Even though circumstances change and new experiences accumulate, memory links those experiences into an evolving narrative.

Yet this continuity can also create constraints.

When certain memories dominate the narrative of identity, individuals may struggle to recognize aspects of themselves that fall outside that narrative. A person who strongly identifies with past failures may overlook evidence of growth and competence. Someone who identifies with past success may underestimate the possibility of change or vulnerability.

In these cases, memory reinforces a version of identity that feels stable but may not fully reflect the individual's present capabilities or possibilities.

Another dimension of memory's influence on identity involves the anticipation of the future.

Individuals rarely think of memory as something that shapes expectations about what lies ahead. Yet the patterns drawn from past experience often guide how people imagine their future. Someone whose memories emphasize opportunity and support may anticipate further opportunities. Someone whose memories emphasize disappointment may anticipate further disappointment.

In this way, memory contributes not only to the narrative of the past but also to the expectations that shape the future.

The self becomes a bridge between what has happened and what might happen next.

This dynamic reveals why identity can feel both stable and evolving at the same time. The narrative of the self provides continuity across time, yet the meaning of that narrative continues to develop as new experiences occur. Each new memory becomes another potential element within the ongoing story of identity.

Within Psychological Architecture, identity represents the domain in which interpretation, emotion, and memory converge into a coherent sense of self. The mind interprets events, emotion signals their significance, and memory preserves those experiences across time. Identity then organizes those elements into a narrative that gives life its psychological structure.

Through this process, the self emerges not as a fixed object but as an evolving story constructed from remembered experience.

Identity as Stability and Constraint

Identity provides one of the most important forms of stability within human psychological life. Without some consistent sense of self, experience would feel fragmented and unpredictable. Individuals would have difficulty understanding their own actions, maintaining commitments, or sustaining relationships across time. Identity offers a framework that allows a person to recognize themselves as the same individual from one moment to the next, even as circumstances change.

This stabilizing function is essential.

When individuals know who they are—or believe they know who they are—they can make decisions with a sense of continuity. They develop expectations about how they will respond to situations and how others will respond to them. This predictability helps reduce uncertainty in everyday life.

Consider how identity shapes ordinary decisions. A person who sees themselves as responsible may feel a natural obligation to fulfill commitments even when doing so requires effort. Someone who identifies strongly as a caregiver may instinctively prioritize the needs of family members. An individual who views themselves as independent may feel compelled to solve problems without relying heavily on others.

In each case, identity acts as a guide for behavior.

Rather than evaluating every possible action from the beginning, individuals often rely on their sense of self to determine what feels appropriate. Identity provides an internal reference point that simplifies decision-making. Actions that align with the identity narrative feel natural or authentic. Actions that contradict that narrative may feel uncomfortable or inconsistent with the person's character.

This sense of internal consistency helps maintain psychological stability.

When individuals act in ways that align with their identity, they experience a sense of coherence between who they believe themselves to be and how they behave in the world. This coherence contributes to feelings of authenticity and self-trust. It allows people to navigate complex social environments without constantly questioning their role or purpose.

Yet the same stability that identity provides can also create limitations.

Because identity organizes experience into a coherent narrative, it tends to resist information that threatens that narrative. Individuals often feel discomfort when confronted with evidence that contradicts their sense of self. This discomfort can lead them to reinterpret events in ways that preserve the existing identity.

For example, someone who believes they are consistently competent may struggle to acknowledge mistakes. Rather than revising their identity, they may attribute the mistake to unusual circumstances or to the actions of others. Conversely, someone who believes they are inadequate may discount their successes as luck or coincidence rather than revising the narrative of limitation.

In both cases, identity shapes how new experiences are interpreted.

This process helps explain why identity can become resistant to change even when individuals encounter experiences that challenge their assumptions. The narrative structure of identity seeks coherence, and coherence often requires preserving the existing story.

Another way identity can become constraining involves expectations about possibility.

When individuals strongly identify with certain roles or characteristics, they may unconsciously limit the range of futures they consider available. A person who sees themselves as "not the kind of person who takes risks" may avoid opportunities that require bold decisions. Someone who identifies as shy may decline invitations to social situations that could expand their sense of connection.

These limitations do not necessarily arise from external barriers. They arise from the narrative boundaries individuals place around themselves.

Identity can therefore function as both a source of direction and a set of invisible constraints.

The stabilizing influence of identity becomes particularly visible during periods of change. When individuals encounter experiences that challenge their established sense of self—such as a career transition, a significant relationship change, or an unexpected life event—they may experience a sense of disorientation.

The narrative that once provided coherence may no longer fully explain the present circumstances.

For example, someone who has long identified as a successful professional may feel uncertain after losing a job or changing careers. The experience does not merely affect their external situation; it challenges the narrative through which they previously understood themselves. Similarly, a person who has always seen themselves as independent may struggle emotionally when illness or aging requires greater reliance on others.

In such moments, individuals may feel as though the ground beneath their identity has shifted.

These experiences reveal that identity is not simply a static description of who a person is. It is an ongoing narrative that must adapt as circumstances evolve. When the narrative fails to adapt, individuals may feel trapped within a version of themselves that no longer reflects their lived experience.

Yet when identity remains flexible, it can incorporate new experiences and expand rather than contract.

Someone who once saw themselves as shy may gradually integrate new experiences of confidence into their identity narrative. A person who once defined themselves primarily through professional achievement may discover additional sources of meaning in relationships, creativity, or service.

In these cases, identity evolves while maintaining continuity with the past.

This capacity for adaptation is essential because human lives are rarely linear. Individuals encounter unexpected opportunities, losses, and transformations throughout the lifespan. An identity narrative that remains too rigid may struggle to incorporate these changes, while a narrative that remains flexible can grow alongside them.

Within Psychological Architecture, identity therefore occupies a complex position.

It stabilizes the psychological system by providing continuity and coherence. At the same time, it can constrain perception and possibility when the narrative becomes too rigid. The balance between stability and flexibility determines whether identity functions as a supportive framework or a limiting structure.

Understanding this balance allows individuals to recognize that the story they carry about themselves is not simply a description of the past. It is an evolving narrative that continues to shape how life unfolds.

Identity provides continuity within the psychological system, but identity alone cannot fully orient a life. The narratives individuals construct about themselves are always embedded within broader questions about purpose, value, and direction. When identity becomes uncertain, individuals often experience not only confusion about who they are but also uncertainty about what their lives are meant to mean. For this reason, identity must ultimately be understood in relation to a wider horizon of significance. That horizon is the domain of meaning.

***

5

Meaning: The Integrating Structure

Human beings do not only experience events. They ask what those events mean.

This tendency appears in nearly every aspect of psychological life. When people face difficulty, they often ask why it happened. When they achieve something important, they ask what the accomplishment represents. When relationships change or life circumstances shift, individuals naturally attempt to understand how those experiences fit into the broader story of their lives.

These questions reveal a dimension of psychological life that extends beyond interpretation, emotional response, and identity. Individuals are not satisfied simply knowing what happened or how they feel about it. They want to understand the larger significance of their experiences.

This search for significance is what we refer to as meaning.

Meaning operates as the integrating structure within Psychological Architecture. While the mind interprets events, emotion regulates responses, and identity organizes experience into a narrative of the self, meaning connects that narrative to a broader framework of purpose and value. It answers a different kind of question than the other domains.

Identity asks, Who am I?

Meaning asks, Why does my life matter?

This distinction may appear subtle at first, yet it represents an important shift in perspective. Identity organizes the story of the individual, but meaning places that story within a larger context. It allows individuals to see their experiences not only as personal events but as part of a broader pattern of significance.

People often become most aware of this domain during moments of transition or uncertainty. A career change, the loss of a loved one, the birth of a child, or a major personal achievement may prompt reflection about the direction of one's life. Individuals may begin asking questions that extend beyond immediate circumstances.

What am I trying to build with my life?

What values guide my decisions?

What matters enough to justify the effort and difficulty of living?

These questions reveal that human beings are not only practical problem-solvers. They are also meaning-seeking creatures.

The search for meaning is not limited to philosophical reflection. It appears in everyday choices about work, relationships, commitments, and goals. When individuals decide how to spend their time or energy, they are implicitly making judgments about what matters. These judgments form the foundation of meaning within their lives.

For example, someone who devotes substantial effort to caring for family members may interpret that commitment as an expression of love and responsibility. Another person who dedicates their time to creative work may experience meaning through expression and contribution. Someone who pursues social change may derive meaning from the belief that their actions can improve the lives of others.

In each case, meaning arises from the relationship between actions and values.

Values represent the principles or ideals that individuals believe are worth pursuing. Meaning emerges when life experiences align with those values. When individuals feel that their actions reflect what matters most to them, their lives acquire a sense of direction and coherence that extends beyond momentary emotional states.

This sense of direction can be powerful. It allows individuals to endure difficulty and uncertainty because those experiences appear connected to something worthwhile. Effort becomes easier to sustain when it serves a purpose that feels meaningful.

Meaning therefore performs an integrative function within the architecture of human experience.

Interpretation, emotion, and identity all contribute to the formation of meaning. The mind interprets events and recognizes patterns. Emotion signals the significance of those events. Identity organizes experiences into a coherent narrative about the self. Meaning then connects that narrative to values, purposes, and goals that extend beyond the individual moment.

Through this process, the events of life become part of a larger framework of significance.

Yet meaning does not arise automatically from experience. Individuals must interpret their lives in ways that connect personal narratives to broader values or purposes. Without this connection, experiences may feel fragmented or directionless.

Consider the difference between two individuals performing the same task. One person may view the task as meaningless routine, something required only to meet external expectations. Another person may view the same activity as part of a larger purpose, such as supporting a family, contributing to a community, or developing mastery in a chosen field.

The external behavior may appear identical, but the psychological experience differs dramatically because the interpretation of meaning differs.

Meaning therefore transforms the subjective experience of life.

When individuals experience meaning in their actions, effort can feel worthwhile even when circumstances are difficult. Challenges may appear as part of a meaningful journey rather than as pointless obstacles. When meaning is absent, even comfortable circumstances may feel empty or unsatisfying.

This contrast helps explain why people often continue searching for meaning even when basic needs are satisfied. Comfort alone rarely produces lasting fulfillment. Individuals tend to feel most alive when their actions connect to something they consider significant.

Within Psychological Architecture, meaning represents the domain in which the other three domains find their ultimate orientation. Interpretation identifies what is happening, emotion signals its importance, identity organizes it into a narrative, and meaning answers the larger question of why that narrative matters.

Through meaning, the architecture of human experience extends beyond the individual moment and toward the broader horizon of purpose and value.

Why Human Beings Search for Meaning

The human search for meaning is so common that it often goes unnoticed. People ask questions about purpose and significance in quiet ways throughout their lives. They wonder whether their work matters, whether their relationships are meaningful, and whether the effort they invest in their daily lives contributes to something worthwhile. These questions do not arise only during moments of crisis. They are present, sometimes subtly and sometimes urgently, whenever individuals reflect on the direction of their lives.

This tendency to search for meaning appears across cultures and historical periods. Different societies offer different answers to questions of purpose, yet the questions themselves remain remarkably consistent. Human beings seem naturally inclined to look beyond the immediate moment and ask what their experiences ultimately represent.

Part of this inclination arises from the way the human mind organizes time. People do not live entirely in the present moment. They remember the past and anticipate the future. Experiences are rarely understood as isolated events; instead, they are placed within a broader timeline that connects what has happened, what is happening, and what might happen next.

Because individuals experience life across time, they seek coherence within that timeline. They want to understand how the past led to the present and how the present might shape the future. Meaning provides the interpretive structure that allows life to appear as a coherent progression rather than as a sequence of disconnected events.

Without such coherence, experience can feel disorienting. A person may accomplish many tasks and move through daily routines yet still feel uncertain about what those activities represent. When actions appear unrelated to a larger purpose, they may begin to feel empty or mechanical.

Meaning transforms activity into direction.

This transformation is visible in many areas of life. Work, for example, may be experienced very differently depending on whether individuals view their efforts as meaningful. A person who believes their work contributes to something important may approach the same tasks with greater engagement and persistence than someone who experiences those tasks as pointless obligations.

Relationships operate in a similar way. Individuals who see their relationships as expressions of commitment, care, and shared purpose often experience those connections as deeply meaningful. When relationships appear transactional or temporary, they may feel less significant even if they involve similar activities.

Meaning therefore changes the psychological experience of life even when external circumstances remain the same.

Another reason human beings search for meaning lies in the emotional dimension of experience. As discussed earlier, emotional signals highlight what appears significant. Joy, grief, pride, love, and disappointment all signal that certain experiences matter deeply to the individual.

When people encounter strong emotional experiences, they often attempt to interpret those emotions within a larger framework of significance. After a painful loss, individuals may search for ways to understand what the relationship meant and how the experience fits into the story of their lives. After a moment of success or achievement, they may reflect on the effort and growth that led to that moment.

Emotion invites reflection about meaning because emotional experiences signal that something important has occurred.

The search for meaning also arises from the uniquely human capacity for self-awareness. People do not simply act; they can observe themselves acting. They can reflect on their motivations, evaluate their decisions, and imagine alternative possibilities. This reflective capacity allows individuals to step back from immediate circumstances and ask broader questions about the direction of their lives.

Self-awareness therefore expands the scope of psychological experience. Instead of responding only to immediate needs, individuals can consider long-term goals, values, and purposes. They can ask whether their actions align with what they believe matters most.

This reflective capacity explains why individuals sometimes feel compelled to reconsider the course of their lives. A person may reach a point where they ask whether their current path reflects their values or aspirations. These moments of reflection often lead to significant changes in career, relationships, or personal priorities.

Such decisions are rarely driven by external circumstances alone. They often arise from a growing sense that the individual's life no longer aligns with the meaning they seek.

Meaning therefore serves as a guiding structure that helps individuals evaluate the direction of their lives. It provides a framework through which choices can be assessed and priorities established.

Another important aspect of the search for meaning involves the human awareness of limitation. People recognize that their time and energy are finite. Life contains uncertainty, loss, and change. This awareness often intensifies the desire to ensure that one's efforts contribute to something worthwhile.

When individuals feel that their lives serve a purpose beyond momentary satisfaction, they may experience a sense of fulfillment even during periods of difficulty. Effort, sacrifice, and persistence can appear meaningful when they contribute to goals or values that extend beyond the present moment.

Without such a framework, challenges may appear pointless rather than purposeful.

The search for meaning therefore represents more than a philosophical curiosity. It is a fundamental aspect of how human beings organize their psychological lives. Meaning allows individuals to interpret their experiences within a broader structure of significance. It connects past events, present actions, and future aspirations into a coherent framework.

Within Psychological Architecture, this domain represents the point at which the other domains converge. Interpretation provides the understanding of events, emotion signals their importance, and identity organizes them into the story of the self. Meaning then situates that story within a larger context of values and purpose.

Through this process, human life becomes more than a sequence of experiences. It becomes a narrative oriented toward significance.

Meaning, Values, and Direction

Meaning does not arise from experience alone. It emerges from the relationship between experience and values. Values represent the principles, commitments, or ideals that individuals consider important enough to guide their lives. When people believe their actions reflect what they value, their experiences begin to feel purposeful. Without this alignment, even significant achievements may feel hollow or disconnected.

Values therefore act as the organizing center of meaning.

Individuals rarely move through life without some sense of what matters to them. These priorities may not always be articulated explicitly, yet they influence countless decisions. People choose careers, friendships, communities, and daily habits in ways that reflect underlying judgments about what is worthwhile. Even when individuals feel uncertain about their direction, they often possess implicit values that shape their preferences and motivations.

Some values are oriented toward relationships. People may believe that caring for others, maintaining loyalty, or supporting family members represents the most important work they can do. Others may prioritize creativity, independence, knowledge, or achievement. Still others may devote their lives to spiritual commitments, community service, or the pursuit of justice.

None of these values exists in isolation from experience. They develop gradually as individuals encounter situations that reveal what feels significant or fulfilling. Moments of connection may reinforce the importance of loyalty or love. Experiences of growth may strengthen the value placed on learning or creativity. Encounters with injustice may intensify a commitment to fairness or social responsibility.

Over time, these values begin to shape the direction of a person's life.

Direction emerges when individuals organize their actions around what they consider meaningful. Instead of responding only to immediate circumstances, they begin making decisions that reflect long-term commitments. A person who values compassion may choose work that allows them to support others. Someone who values discovery may pursue research or exploration. Someone who values family may organize their priorities around sustaining relationships.

Meaning grows when these values are expressed through action.

This alignment between values and behavior often produces a sense of coherence. Individuals feel that their efforts contribute to something they consider worthwhile. Challenges and sacrifices appear justified because they serve goals that extend beyond momentary comfort.

Consider how differently two individuals might experience the same demanding responsibility. One person may see the work as burdensome, something endured only to meet external expectations. Another may interpret the same responsibility as an opportunity to serve a value they hold deeply, such as caring for others or contributing to a community. The external task may remain identical, but the psychological experience differs because the meaning attached to the work differs.

Meaning therefore transforms effort into purpose.

Yet values do more than create direction. They also help individuals navigate uncertainty. Life rarely unfolds in predictable ways. Unexpected changes, setbacks, and opportunities frequently alter the path individuals imagined for themselves. In such moments, values provide a stable reference point that helps guide decisions even when circumstances shift.

A person who values honesty may remain committed to truthful communication even during difficult conversations. Someone who values creativity may continue pursuing expression even when practical challenges arise. These values function as anchors that help maintain direction when external conditions change.

At the same time, individuals often carry multiple values that compete for attention. A person may value professional success while also valuing family life and personal well-being. These commitments may sometimes conflict, requiring choices about how time and energy will be allocated.

Such tensions are not signs of failure within the system of meaning. They reflect the complexity of human life. Individuals continually adjust their priorities as circumstances evolve, attempting to balance competing values in ways that feel coherent.

The process of negotiating these tensions contributes to the development of a meaningful life. As individuals reflect on what matters most to them, they gradually refine the values that guide their decisions.

Meaning therefore develops through ongoing reflection and engagement with experience. It is not something discovered once and permanently resolved. Instead, individuals continually revise their understanding of what matters as they encounter new relationships, responsibilities, and possibilities.

Within Psychological Architecture, this evolving alignment between values and action represents the core of the domain of meaning. Interpretation allows individuals to understand their experiences, emotion signals their importance, and identity organizes those experiences into a narrative of the self. Meaning then connects that narrative to values that provide direction and significance.

Through this connection, the architecture of human experience acquires orientation. Life becomes organized not only by what has happened but also by what individuals believe is worth pursuing.

When Meaning Breaks Down

The experience of meaning often feels stable when life unfolds in familiar ways. Individuals pursue goals, maintain relationships, and follow routines that align with their values. The direction of life may feel clear, even if it is not consciously examined very often. Meaning operates quietly in the background, organizing choices and providing a sense that one's efforts contribute to something worthwhile.

Yet there are moments when this sense of meaning begins to weaken or disappear.

These moments can be deeply unsettling because meaning functions as the integrative structure of psychological life. When individuals lose confidence in the significance of their actions, the coherence that once guided their decisions may begin to dissolve. Activities that once felt purposeful may start to feel mechanical or empty.

Meaning does not always break down suddenly. Often it erodes gradually.

A person may begin to notice that routines once experienced as fulfilling no longer produce the same sense of engagement. Work that once felt meaningful may begin to feel repetitive or disconnected from deeper values. Relationships may continue outwardly unchanged while internally losing the sense of purpose that once sustained them.

These shifts may occur without any obvious external event. From the outside, life may appear stable. Yet internally the individual begins to question whether the direction of their life still reflects what matters most to them.

In other cases, the breakdown of meaning occurs during periods of significant change.

Major life transitions often disrupt the structures that previously provided a sense of purpose. The loss of a loved one, the end of a relationship, the loss of employment, or a sudden change in health can all challenge the assumptions through which individuals previously understood their lives. When these events occur, the narrative of identity may remain intact while the meaning attached to that narrative begins to feel uncertain.

For example, someone who has devoted decades to a career may experience disorientation when that career suddenly ends. The routines, goals, and relationships associated with that role may have provided a strong sense of meaning. When those structures disappear, the individual may struggle to identify what now gives direction to their life.

Similarly, a person who has organized their life around caring for others may face a period of uncertainty when those responsibilities change. The values that once guided their daily actions remain important, but the context in which those values were expressed may no longer exist in the same form.

In such moments individuals may experience a feeling often described as emptiness or disconnection. Activities that once carried clear significance may begin to feel arbitrary. Effort may seem difficult to justify because the larger framework that once gave those efforts meaning has weakened.

This experience is sometimes described as a crisis of meaning.

Yet the breakdown of meaning does not always arise from loss or disruption. It can also emerge from success.

Individuals who achieve goals that once seemed central to their sense of purpose may discover that the accomplishment does not provide the lasting fulfillment they expected. After reaching the milestone, they may begin asking new questions about what their life should represent moving forward.

In these cases, the previous framework of meaning may have been tied too narrowly to a particular achievement. Once the goal is reached, the individual must reconsider how their life connects to broader values or purposes.

Another way meaning can break down involves the tension between identity and experience. If individuals continue acting in ways that no longer align with their deeper values, the resulting disconnect may gradually weaken their sense of purpose. The narrative of identity may remain stable, but the meaning attached to that narrative begins to feel uncertain.

For example, someone who once valued creativity may find themselves working in environments that discourage expression or innovation. Over time, the individual may begin to feel disconnected from the values that once gave their life direction. Even if external success remains intact, the absence of alignment between values and action may produce a sense of dissatisfaction.

These experiences illustrate that meaning cannot be sustained through routine alone. It depends on an ongoing relationship between values, actions, and interpretation.

When that relationship weakens, individuals often begin searching for ways to restore coherence. They may reconsider their priorities, seek new relationships, explore different forms of work, or reflect more deeply on what they believe matters most.

While these periods can be uncomfortable, they also represent important moments within psychological life. The breakdown of meaning often signals that the existing framework no longer fully reflects the individual's evolving values or circumstances.

In this sense, the loss of meaning can create the conditions for its renewal.

When individuals begin questioning the direction of their lives, they open the possibility of constructing a new relationship between identity and purpose. This process requires reflection, experimentation, and sometimes the willingness to revise long-held assumptions about who they are and what their lives represent.

Within Psychological Architecture, the breakdown of meaning represents a disruption in the integrative structure that connects interpretation, emotion, and identity. When that structure weakens, individuals may feel uncertain about how their experiences fit into a coherent framework of significance.

Yet this disruption does not mark the end of meaning. It marks the moment when the search for meaning becomes conscious.

Rebuilding Meaning

When the sense of meaning in a person's life begins to weaken, the experience can feel disorienting. Activities that once seemed purposeful may no longer feel connected to anything larger. Decisions that once appeared straightforward may suddenly seem uncertain. The individual may feel as though the structure that once organized their efforts has dissolved.

Yet the loss of meaning does not leave individuals without resources. The same psychological architecture that allowed meaning to form in the first place also provides the foundation for rebuilding it.

Rebuilding meaning rarely begins with a single insight. Instead, it unfolds gradually as individuals reconsider how their experiences connect to what they value most. This process often begins with reflection. When the routines and assumptions that once guided life no longer provide direction, individuals may begin asking deeper questions about what truly matters to them.

These questions are not always comfortable. They may challenge long-held assumptions about success, identity, or obligation. Yet they also create the possibility of constructing a more authentic relationship between one's actions and one's values.

Reflection alone, however, does not restore meaning. Meaning emerges when reflection leads to engagement with life in new ways. Individuals often begin experimenting with different forms of action that align more closely with their evolving sense of purpose. They may explore new work, strengthen relationships that reflect their values, or pursue activities that express creativity, service, or curiosity.

Through these actions, meaning begins to reappear.

This process reflects an important feature of the domain of meaning: it is not purely conceptual. Meaning does not arise only from thinking about life. It arises from living in ways that express what one believes matters. When actions align with values, individuals often experience a renewed sense that their efforts contribute to something significant.

Consider someone who has experienced a loss that disrupted the meaning structure of their life. In the early stages, the individual may feel disconnected from activities that once seemed purposeful. Over time, however, they may begin finding meaning through new forms of connection, such as supporting others who face similar experiences or investing more deeply in relationships that remain important.

The values that once guided their life do not disappear. Instead, they find new expressions.

Another person may rebuild meaning after realizing that their previous goals no longer reflect what they value most. A career that once represented success may begin to feel misaligned with deeper priorities. In response, the individual may gradually shift their efforts toward work or commitments that better express those values.

Such changes rarely occur instantly. Rebuilding meaning often requires patience as individuals test new directions and integrate those experiences into their identity narrative.

Throughout this process, the other domains of Psychological Architecture remain deeply involved. The mind interprets new experiences and recognizes emerging patterns. Emotion signals when those experiences resonate with deeper values. Identity begins to incorporate new chapters into the story of the self.

Meaning then integrates these elements into a renewed sense of direction.

This integration explains why meaning often becomes stronger after periods of uncertainty. When individuals consciously examine what matters to them, the resulting commitments may feel more authentic than those that emerged through habit or external expectation.

Meaning constructed through reflection and engagement tends to feel more resilient because it reflects the individual's evolving understanding of their life.

Another important aspect of rebuilding meaning involves recognizing that purpose rarely appears as a single, permanent answer. Human lives unfold across changing circumstances, and the sources of meaning often evolve as individuals encounter new experiences.

What gives meaning to life during early adulthood may differ from what feels meaningful later in life. Responsibilities shift, relationships deepen, and priorities evolve. Rather than searching for a single fixed purpose, individuals often find meaning by remaining attentive to how their values continue expressing themselves across different stages of life.

Meaning therefore functions less like a destination and more like an orientation.

It provides direction rather than a final endpoint. Individuals move through life guided by values that give their experiences coherence and significance. Even when circumstances change, those values can find new forms of expression.

Within Psychological Architecture, meaning represents the domain that integrates the entire system. The mind interprets events, emotion signals their importance, and identity organizes those experiences into the story of the self. Meaning then connects that story to values and purposes that extend beyond the individual moment.

Through this integration, the architecture of human experience becomes complete.

Life is no longer understood only as a sequence of events or as the unfolding of a personal narrative. It becomes a journey oriented toward significance, shaped by the values individuals choose to express through their actions.

* * *

6

Structural Instability: When Psychological Systems Begin to Fracture

Most of the time, the architecture of human experience operates quietly in the background of life. The mind interprets events, emotion signals their significance, identity organizes those experiences into a narrative, and meaning connects that narrative to values and direction. When these domains interact smoothly, individuals experience a sense of psychological coherence. Life may contain challenges and uncertainty, but the overall structure of experience remains stable enough for people to move forward with confidence.

Yet there are periods when this stability begins to weaken.

During such times, individuals may feel as though the internal structure that once organized their lives is no longer functioning in the same way. Situations that once felt manageable may suddenly appear overwhelming. Emotional responses may become unusually intense or difficult to regulate. Long-held assumptions about identity or purpose may begin to feel uncertain.

These experiences are often described as periods of psychological instability.

Instability does not necessarily mean that something is wrong with the individual. In many cases it reflects the natural strain placed on the architecture of experience when the demands of life exceed the system's current capacity for integration. Just as physical structures can become unstable when they encounter forces beyond their design limits, psychological structures may struggle when interpretations, emotions, identity narratives, and meaning frameworks begin to conflict with one another.

Understanding this process requires looking again at how the four domains interact.

The mind interprets events by assigning meaning to what is happening. Emotion regulates the individual's response to those interpretations. Identity organizes experiences into a narrative that provides continuity across time. Meaning connects that narrative to values and purpose.

When these domains remain aligned, experience tends to feel coherent. Interpretation supports emotional regulation. Emotional signals reinforce the identity narrative. Identity aligns with values that give life direction.

Instability begins to emerge when this alignment weakens.

For example, the mind may begin interpreting events in ways that produce emotional responses the individual struggles to regulate. Anxiety may increase as the mind repeatedly anticipates threat. Anger may intensify when interpretations focus on perceived injustice or violation. Sadness may deepen when events appear to confirm a narrative of loss or inadequacy.

As emotional activation increases, attention often narrows around the signals associated with that emotion. Anxiety focuses attention on potential dangers. Anger focuses attention on perceived offenses. Sadness focuses attention on themes of disappointment or loss.

This narrowing of attention influences how new experiences are interpreted.

When the emotional system is strongly activated, the mind may begin interpreting events in ways that reinforce the existing emotional state. Neutral situations may be perceived as threatening, critical, or discouraging depending on the dominant emotional signal. The interpretive engine begins to organize perception around the emotion already present.

At the same time, identity may begin to adapt to these repeated experiences. If an individual repeatedly interprets events as threatening and experiences persistent anxiety, they may begin incorporating those patterns into the story they tell about themselves. They may start viewing themselves as someone who is constantly under pressure or someone who struggles to cope with uncertainty.

Once such narratives become part of identity, they can reinforce the interpretive patterns that produced them.

Meaning may also become affected during periods of instability. When experiences repeatedly conflict with a person's expectations about how life should unfold, the values and purposes that once provided direction may begin to feel uncertain. Individuals may question whether their efforts lead to anything worthwhile or whether the goals they have pursued still reflect what matters most to them.

When meaning weakens, the architecture loses one of its most important sources of integration.

The result is often a sense of fragmentation. Individuals may feel pulled in different directions by conflicting interpretations, emotional responses, and identity narratives. Decisions become more difficult because the values that once guided those decisions no longer feel clear.

Yet instability does not arise only during periods of difficulty. It can also emerge during periods of rapid growth or transition.

When individuals encounter experiences that expand their sense of possibility, the existing architecture may struggle to incorporate those changes. A new opportunity may challenge the identity narrative a person has held for years. A major achievement may require revising beliefs about what is possible in the future. Even positive changes can create instability if the psychological structure must reorganize itself to accommodate them.

For example, someone who has long seen themselves as cautious and reserved may find their identity challenged by unexpected success or recognition. The experience may conflict with the narrative they previously held about their abilities. Integrating this new reality may require adjusting interpretations, emotional responses, and expectations about the future.

Such moments illustrate that instability often accompanies transformation.

Psychological systems, like many complex systems, sometimes become unstable when they are in the process of reorganizing themselves. The discomfort associated with instability may therefore represent the beginning of change rather than the failure of the system.

Understanding instability in structural terms helps clarify why certain patterns tend to emerge during these periods.

When the architecture of experience becomes strained, individuals often attempt to restore stability by relying more heavily on familiar interpretations and behaviors. The mind may cling to established narratives even when those narratives no longer fully explain current circumstances. Emotional responses may become more reactive as the system attempts to regain equilibrium.

These attempts at stabilization can sometimes create repeating patterns within the psychological system.

For instance, someone experiencing anxiety may begin avoiding situations that trigger discomfort. Avoidance provides temporary relief, but it also prevents the individual from encountering experiences that might revise the interpretation generating the anxiety. Over time the avoidance pattern reinforces the belief that the situation is genuinely dangerous.

Similarly, someone whose identity is strongly tied to competence may respond defensively to feedback that challenges that identity. Rather than revising the narrative, the individual may dismiss the feedback or interpret it as unfair criticism. This response preserves the identity narrative in the short term but may prevent learning that would strengthen the system in the long term.

These examples illustrate how instability can produce self-reinforcing patterns.

The psychological system attempts to restore coherence by repeating familiar interpretations and responses. Yet these repetitions may prevent the architecture from adapting to new conditions.

Recognizing instability as a structural phenomenon helps shift the perspective through which such experiences are understood. Rather than viewing emotional distress or identity conflict as isolated problems, it becomes possible to see them as signals that the architecture of experience is under strain.

These signals invite closer examination of how interpretation, emotion, identity, and meaning are interacting.

Periods of instability often mark the moments when individuals become most aware of the underlying structure of their psychological lives. The patterns that once operated quietly in the background become visible because they no longer produce the stability they once provided.

In this way, instability can serve as a doorway to deeper understanding.

When individuals begin examining how their interpretations shape emotional responses, how emotional experiences influence identity narratives, and how those narratives connect to meaning, they gain the opportunity to reorganize the architecture of their experience.

Such reorganization rarely occurs instantly. It unfolds gradually as individuals experiment with new interpretations, confront avoided experiences, revise identity narratives, and reconnect with values that provide direction.

Through this process, instability becomes part of the system's capacity for change rather than merely a sign of breakdown.

The Dynamics of Psychological Strain

Structural instability rarely appears without warning. In most cases, the architecture of experience begins showing subtle signs of strain before a full sense of disruption emerges. Individuals may notice shifts in emotional intensity, changes in interpretation, or growing uncertainty about the direction of their lives. These signals often appear gradually, sometimes so quietly that they are easy to overlook.

At the center of this process lies the interaction between interpretation and emotional regulation.

When the mind begins interpreting events in ways that repeatedly signal threat, loss, or failure, the emotional system responds by mobilizing states associated with those interpretations. Anxiety may increase when the mind anticipates danger. Frustration may intensify when the mind repeatedly perceives obstacles or injustice. Sadness may deepen when interpretations emphasize disappointment or loss.

These emotional responses, in turn, influence how the mind interprets subsequent experiences.

Emotion narrows attention toward signals that appear consistent with the current emotional state. A person experiencing anxiety becomes more sensitive to potential risks or uncertainties. Someone experiencing anger becomes more attentive to signs of disrespect or unfairness. When sadness dominates, the mind may focus on memories or interpretations that reinforce themes of disappointment.

Over time, this interaction can create a feedback loop between interpretation and emotion.

The mind interprets events in ways that trigger emotional activation. Emotional activation then influences which aspects of experience receive attention. Those aspects reinforce the interpretation that generated the emotional response in the first place.

Within a stable psychological system, this loop remains flexible. New experiences provide opportunities for the interpretive engine to update its assumptions. Emotional states shift as circumstances change, and the identity narrative integrates these experiences into a coherent story.

During periods of strain, however, this flexibility may begin to diminish.

The mind may become increasingly confident in particular interpretations even when those interpretations no longer fully reflect present conditions. Emotional responses may persist long after the events that triggered them have passed. Identity narratives may begin organizing new experiences around themes that reinforce the existing emotional pattern.

As this process unfolds, individuals may feel trapped within a cycle that seems difficult to interrupt.

For example, someone who begins interpreting ambiguous situations as threatening may experience increasing anxiety. The anxiety encourages avoidance of those situations, which prevents the individual from encountering evidence that might challenge the interpretation. Because the mind never receives new information that contradicts the expectation of danger, the interpretive pattern grows stronger.

Similarly, someone who repeatedly interprets interpersonal interactions as disrespectful may experience persistent anger. The emotional response may lead to confrontational behavior that strains relationships. When those relationships deteriorate, the individual may interpret the outcome as confirmation that others are indeed hostile or unfair.

In both cases, the architecture of experience becomes organized around a reinforcing pattern.

These patterns do not arise from weakness or lack of effort. They emerge from the way the psychological system attempts to maintain coherence during periods of strain. When uncertainty increases, the system often gravitates toward interpretations that feel familiar. Familiar interpretations create a sense of predictability even when they produce emotional distress.

Another important aspect of psychological strain involves the role of identity.

Identity narratives help individuals maintain continuity across time. When experiences begin challenging the assumptions embedded within those narratives, individuals may feel a sense of threat that extends beyond the immediate situation. The experience may feel as though it questions who they are rather than merely presenting a practical problem.

For instance, a person who strongly identifies with competence may experience intense discomfort when confronted with repeated setbacks. The setbacks do not simply represent obstacles to overcome; they appear to challenge the narrative that defines the individual's sense of self.

Similarly, someone who identifies strongly with independence may struggle deeply when circumstances require them to rely on others. The emotional strain arises not only from the practical difficulty of the situation but from the perceived threat to the identity narrative itself.

When identity becomes intertwined with particular interpretations of experience, the psychological system may resist information that requires revising that narrative.

This resistance can amplify strain because the architecture of experience must accommodate realities that no longer fit the existing structure. The system attempts to preserve coherence by defending the narrative, yet the experiences themselves continue challenging it.

Meaning may also become unstable during periods of strain.

When individuals encounter repeated experiences that conflict with their expectations about how life should unfold, the values and purposes that once provided direction may begin to feel uncertain. Efforts that once appeared meaningful may start to feel disconnected from a larger sense of purpose.

In these moments individuals often begin asking questions that reach beyond the immediate circumstances. They may wonder whether the goals they have pursued still reflect what matters most to them. They may question whether the path they have followed continues to provide direction.

Such questioning can feel unsettling because it suggests that the architecture organizing one's life may require revision.

Yet this questioning also represents the beginning of a deeper process. When individuals become aware of the patterns shaping their interpretations, emotional responses, identity narratives, and sources of meaning, they gain the opportunity to examine how those patterns developed.

This awareness does not immediately resolve the strain within the system. However, it introduces the possibility of change. By recognizing the dynamics through which the architecture of experience has become strained, individuals can begin exploring alternative interpretations, emotional responses, and identity narratives that better reflect their current circumstances.

Through this process, the system gradually regains flexibility.

Psychological strain therefore represents a moment when the architecture of experience reveals its internal dynamics. The patterns that once operated invisibly become visible because they no longer produce stability.

This visibility, while uncomfortable, opens the door to a deeper understanding of how the structure of psychological life can reorganize itself.

Reinforcing Loops Within the Psychological System

When the architecture of human experience begins to strain, patterns often emerge that reinforce themselves over time. These patterns are not deliberate strategies chosen by the individual. Instead, they arise from the interaction between interpretation, emotion, identity, and meaning. Each domain influences the others, and when those influences align in particular ways, they can create loops that sustain the very conditions that produced them.

These loops are one of the most important dynamics within Psychological Architecture.

To understand how they form, it is helpful to return to the role of interpretation. The mind constantly attempts to organize experience into patterns that make sense of what is happening. When a particular interpretation appears repeatedly to explain events, the mind becomes increasingly confident in that interpretation. It begins to treat the pattern not as a possibility but as an expectation.

Once an expectation forms, emotional responses begin aligning with it.

If the mind expects threat, anxiety becomes more likely to arise. If the mind anticipates rejection, emotional sensitivity to signs of disapproval increases. If the mind predicts failure, discouragement or hesitation may appear even before a situation unfolds.

Emotion then shapes attention.

Anxious individuals become more attentive to signals that appear dangerous. Someone anticipating rejection becomes highly sensitive to subtle cues in social interaction. Someone expecting failure may focus on potential mistakes while overlooking evidence of progress.

The narrowing of attention reinforces the original interpretation.

Because attention is directed toward signals that confirm the expectation, the mind receives information that appears to validate the pattern it already believes. The individual may conclude that their interpretation was accurate all along. Over time the interpretive pattern becomes increasingly stable because it appears to explain experience consistently.

Identity then begins incorporating this pattern into the narrative of the self.

Someone who repeatedly experiences anxiety in uncertain situations may begin describing themselves as "an anxious person." Someone who frequently encounters interpersonal conflict may begin viewing themselves as someone who "doesn't get along with others." These descriptions may initially arise from specific experiences, but once they become part of identity, they begin shaping future interpretations.

Identity transforms patterns of experience into characteristics of the self.

When individuals begin interpreting their experiences through these identity narratives, they often behave in ways that reinforce the pattern further. A person who believes they are socially awkward may avoid conversations that feel uncertain. Someone who sees themselves as incapable of leadership may hesitate to take initiative in group settings.

Avoidance and hesitation reduce opportunities for experiences that might challenge the narrative.

As a result, the original interpretation remains intact. The absence of contradictory experiences strengthens the sense that the identity narrative accurately reflects reality. Over time, the reinforcing loop becomes increasingly stable.

Meaning may also become involved in these loops.

If individuals begin interpreting their lives through narratives of limitation or failure, they may gradually lose a sense of direction. Activities that once felt purposeful may begin to appear pointless because the individual no longer believes their efforts will produce meaningful outcomes. The weakening of meaning further reduces motivation to explore new possibilities.

In this way, the entire architecture of experience can become organized around a reinforcing pattern.

Interpretation generates expectations.

Emotion amplifies those expectations.

Identity incorporates them into the story of the self.

Meaning adjusts to the perceived limitations of that story.

The system becomes self-consistent even when the underlying interpretation is incomplete or inaccurate.

It is important to recognize that reinforcing loops do not always produce negative outcomes. The same dynamics can support growth and resilience when the patterns involved encourage exploration and learning.

For example, someone who interprets challenges as opportunities for development may experience excitement rather than fear when encountering new situations. Emotional responses of curiosity or determination direct attention toward learning rather than avoidance. Successful experiences then become part of the identity narrative, reinforcing the belief that the individual is capable of growth.

Meaning strengthens this pattern by connecting effort with purpose.

In such cases, reinforcing loops support expansion rather than restriction. The architecture of experience becomes organized around the expectation that new challenges can lead to development.

The difference between restrictive loops and expansive ones lies not in the existence of the loop itself but in the interpretations that initiate it. Because interpretation shapes emotional responses, identity narratives, and meaning structures, small shifts in interpretation can eventually influence the entire system.

Yet recognizing these loops from within the system can be difficult.

When individuals are immersed in a reinforcing pattern, the interpretation guiding that pattern often appears self-evident. Emotional responses feel justified, identity narratives seem accurate, and the resulting behaviors appear natural. From the inside, the loop may simply feel like the way life works.

This is why periods of instability sometimes reveal patterns that previously remained invisible. When the architecture of experience becomes strained, individuals may begin questioning interpretations that once seemed obvious. Emotional responses may appear disproportionate to current circumstances. Identity narratives may begin to feel incomplete or limiting.

Such moments of awareness allow individuals to observe the reinforcing loops that have shaped their experience.

Once these patterns become visible, the possibility of change emerges. By examining the interpretations that initiate emotional responses, individuals can begin experimenting with alternative ways of understanding their experiences. New interpretations can lead to new emotional responses, which create opportunities for different behaviors and identity narratives to develop.

Over time, these changes can alter the direction of the reinforcing loop.

The architecture of experience remains the same, but the patterns moving through it begin shifting. When interpretation becomes more flexible, emotional regulation becomes more adaptable. Identity narratives expand to incorporate new possibilities, and meaning reconnects life with values that encourage growth.

Understanding these reinforcing loops provides a deeper insight into how psychological systems maintain both stability and change.

This book introduces the author's conceptual framework "Psychological Architecture," which organizes human experience into four interacting domains: mind, emotion, identity, and meaning. The work is written for a general audience but engages psychological theory and human development.

When Identity and Meaning Begin to Fracture

As reinforcing loops intensify, the strain within the psychological system often extends beyond interpretation and emotional regulation. Eventually the pressure begins affecting the domains responsible for organizing and integrating experience: identity and meaning.

Identity, as we have seen, provides the narrative structure through which individuals understand themselves across time. Meaning connects that narrative to values and purpose. When instability develops within the system, these two domains may begin to fracture under the weight of conflicting interpretations and emotional patterns.

This fracture does not always appear dramatically at first.

Often the earliest signs are subtle. A person may begin feeling uncertain about decisions that once felt straightforward. Activities that previously seemed aligned with their sense of self may begin to feel strangely disconnected. The narrative through which they once understood their life may start to feel incomplete or unconvincing.

Such moments can create a quiet but persistent sense of unease.

For example, someone who has long identified as confident and capable may begin experiencing repeated setbacks that challenge that narrative. At first the individual may interpret the setbacks as temporary obstacles. But if the pattern continues, the tension between experience and identity may begin to grow.

The individual may find themselves asking questions they never previously considered.

Am I really the person I thought I was?

Have I misunderstood my abilities or direction?

What does this mean for the future I imagined?

These questions signal that the identity narrative is under strain.

Similarly, the domain of meaning may begin weakening when the goals and values that once provided direction no longer appear to produce the expected sense of fulfillment. A career that once felt purposeful may begin to feel routine or empty. A role that once provided strong identity may lose its significance as circumstances change.

When meaning weakens, individuals may begin questioning the significance of their efforts.

Why am I doing this?

Does this actually matter?

Is the direction I have been following still the right one?

These questions often emerge gradually as individuals notice a growing gap between their daily actions and the values that once gave those actions significance.

The fracture between identity and meaning can be particularly destabilizing because these domains provide the highest levels of integration within Psychological Architecture. Interpretation and emotion shape moment-to-moment experience, but identity and meaning organize those experiences into a coherent life story.

When these structures begin weakening, individuals may feel as though their lives have lost direction.

Yet it is important to recognize that this fracture often represents a natural stage within the evolution of the psychological system.

Human lives unfold across changing circumstances. Roles evolve, relationships deepen or dissolve, and values may shift as individuals encounter new experiences. When the architecture of identity and meaning fails to adapt to these changes, strain develops between the narrative individuals carry about themselves and the reality they are living.

The resulting tension often produces a period of psychological questioning.

During this period individuals may revisit earlier interpretations of their experiences. Memories that once supported the identity narrative may be reconsidered in light of new understanding. Emotional responses that once felt automatic may begin to appear less inevitable.

This process can feel uncomfortable because it disrupts the stability that identity and meaning once provided. Yet it also opens the possibility for deeper integration.

When individuals begin questioning the narratives organizing their lives, they gain the opportunity to revise those narratives in ways that better reflect their evolving values and circumstances. The fracture within identity and meaning becomes the starting point for reorganization rather than the collapse of the system.

This reorganization does not occur by abandoning the past entirely. Instead, individuals begin integrating earlier experiences into a broader narrative that acknowledges both continuity and change.

A career setback may become part of a story about learning and redirection rather than failure. A relationship that once defined identity may become one chapter within a larger life narrative rather than its central theme.

Through this process the architecture of identity and meaning begins expanding rather than collapsing.

The individual's sense of self becomes less dependent on a single interpretation of experience. Meaning becomes connected to values that remain stable even as circumstances change. The system regains coherence because its organizing structures become more flexible.

Understanding this process helps explain why periods of psychological strain often precede significant personal growth. When the narratives that once organized experience begin fracturing, individuals are invited to reconsider the foundations of their identity and purpose.

From the perspective of Psychological Architecture, this fracture marks the moment when the system begins preparing for reorganization.

The next stage of the architecture explores how such reorganization becomes possible.

* * *

7

The Structural Models of Psychological Architecture

The preceding chapters described the structural domains through which human experience is organized. Once these domains are understood, recurring patterns begin to emerge in how they interact. Certain forms of psychological tension, adaptation, and change appear repeatedly across different lives and circumstances. Conceptual models help make these patterns visible. The models presented in this chapter therefore illustrate how the domains of mind, emotion, identity, and meaning interact under specific conditions within the architecture of human experience.

By the time individuals begin recognizing the patterns that shape their psychological lives, another realization often follows. These patterns are rarely random. Over time, certain configurations of interpretation, emotion, identity, and meaning appear again and again across different situations. The details of life may vary widely from one person to another, yet the underlying dynamics often follow recognizable structural forms.

These recurring dynamics are what Psychological Architecture describes as structural models.

A structural model does not describe a single behavior or isolated feeling. Instead, it captures a pattern of interaction among the domains of the architecture. It shows how interpretation, emotional regulation, identity

102

organization, and meaning-making can combine to produce a particular psychological pattern that unfolds across time.

When individuals first encounter these models, they often experience a moment of recognition. Situations that once appeared confusing or unpredictable suddenly reveal an underlying structure. What once felt like a series of disconnected emotional reactions begins to look like a coherent pattern operating within the system.

This recognition can be both surprising and relieving.

Much of psychological life unfolds automatically. Interpretations arise quickly, emotions follow those interpretations, identity narratives organize the experience, and meaning provides a broader context through which individuals understand what is happening. Because these processes operate so quickly and continuously, people rarely have the opportunity to step back and observe how the system is functioning as a whole.

Structural models make this observation possible.

They provide a way of seeing the architecture of experience in motion. By identifying the patterns through which the four domains interact, these models allow individuals to recognize the mechanisms shaping their responses to life's challenges and opportunities.

Importantly, these models are not categories of personality or diagnoses of psychological problems. They are patterns of interaction within a system that every human being possesses. The same architectural domains that support resilience and growth can also produce cycles of avoidance, defensive identity narratives, or loss of meaning when the system becomes strained.

The models therefore describe dynamics rather than types of people.

Two individuals may experience the same structural pattern in different ways depending on their circumstances, history, and values. Likewise, the same individual may encounter different patterns at different stages of life. The architecture itself remains constant, but the patterns moving through it may shift as experiences accumulate and interpretations evolve.

Understanding these models also reveals an important principle of Psychological Architecture: complex psychological experiences often arise from relatively simple interactions repeated across time.

A single moment of avoidance may not appear significant. Yet when avoidance becomes the preferred strategy for regulating emotional discomfort, it can gradually shape interpretation, identity, and meaning. Over time, what began as a temporary response may become an organizing pattern within the system.

Similarly, an identity narrative that begins as a small assumption about oneself may gradually expand to influence the interpretation of many experiences. The narrative begins filtering perception, shaping emotional responses, and directing behavior in ways that reinforce the original assumption.

Structural models allow these dynamics to become visible.

By examining how the domains of the architecture interact, individuals can begin recognizing the patterns operating within their own experience. What once appeared to be isolated moments of frustration, anxiety, or uncertainty may reveal themselves as part of a larger structure organizing the system.

This recognition does not immediately change the pattern, but it introduces a new form of awareness.

When individuals can see the structure of a pattern, they are no longer entirely inside it. The interpretive engine of the mind begins noticing the dynamics at work rather than simply reacting to them. Emotional responses may still arise, but they occur within a broader understanding of the system's behavior.

This shift in perspective opens the possibility of change.

Instead of experiencing psychological patterns as mysterious or inevitable, individuals can begin examining how the domains of interpretation, emotion, identity, and meaning interact within their lives. They can explore how certain interpretations lead to particular emotional responses, how identity narratives shape expectations, and how meaning influences the direction of their choices.

In the sections that follow, we will examine several of the structural models that commonly emerge within the architecture of human experience. Each model represents a distinct pattern through which the domains of Psychological Architecture interact.

Understanding these models does not provide a formula for eliminating difficulty from life. Human experience will always include uncertainty, disappointment, and challenge. What these models offer instead is a clearer view of the dynamics through which psychological systems respond to those challenges.

With that clarity, individuals can begin recognizing how the architecture of their experience organizes itself — and how those patterns may gradually evolve over time.

Across many fields of inquiry, complex systems become easier to understand when recurring dynamics are represented through conceptual models. Models do not capture every detail of reality. Instead, they illuminate structural relationships that help explain how certain patterns repeatedly emerge. The models introduced in this chapter serve that function within Psychological Architecture. Each model reveals a recurring dynamic that arises when the domains of mind, emotion, identity, and meaning interact under particular conditions. By examining these patterns, it becomes possible to observe how psychological systems maintain stability, how they become strained under pressure, and how structural change may occur.

The Emotional Avoidance Loop

One of the most common structural patterns within human psychological life emerges when the system begins organizing itself around the avoidance of emotional discomfort. This pattern appears so frequently that many individuals assume it simply reflects ordinary coping behavior. Yet when examined through the lens of Psychological Architecture, a deeper structure becomes visible. Avoidance is not merely a behavior. It becomes a reinforcing loop that gradually shapes interpretation, emotion, identity, and meaning.

To understand this loop, it is helpful to begin with a simple observation about the emotional system. Human beings are naturally motivated to reduce discomfort. When an experience produces anxiety, embarrassment, grief, or shame, the psychological system quickly searches for ways to restore equilibrium. Sometimes this occurs through constructive engagement with the experience. In other cases, the system discovers that avoiding the situation produces faster relief.

That relief is powerful.

When avoidance successfully reduces emotional discomfort, the mind learns something important. It learns that withdrawal, distraction, or disengagement can restore emotional stability more quickly than confronting the underlying experience. Once this learning occurs, the system begins favoring avoidance whenever similar emotional signals arise.

The loop begins with interpretation.

The mind encounters a situation and quickly interprets it as threatening, uncertain, or potentially painful. This interpretation may arise from past experiences, learned expectations, or simply the mind's attempt to anticipate possible outcomes. Once the interpretation is formed, the emotional system activates a corresponding response. Anxiety may appear when uncertainty is interpreted as danger. Shame may arise when the mind anticipates embarrassment or rejection.

The emotional activation creates pressure within the system.

Emotions such as anxiety or shame are designed to draw attention to situations that may require action. Yet these emotions can also feel overwhelming. When the emotional intensity becomes uncomfortable, the system searches for a way to reduce that discomfort.

Avoidance often provides the fastest solution.

An individual may postpone a difficult conversation, withdraw from a challenging opportunity, distract themselves from painful reflection, or leave a situation that produces anxiety. In the short term, this strategy works remarkably well. As soon as the individual withdraws from the source of discomfort, emotional intensity often decreases.

The system experiences relief.

That relief reinforces the behavior that produced it. The mind interprets the reduction of discomfort as evidence that avoidance was the correct response. Because the emotional system has returned to equilibrium, the individual may feel that the problem has been solved.

Yet the underlying interpretation remains unchanged.

The mind continues interpreting the avoided situation as threatening or overwhelming. Because the individual has withdrawn from the experience, the system never encounters new information that might challenge that interpretation. The emotional response therefore remains available, ready to activate the next time a similar situation arises.

This is how the loop forms.

Interpretation identifies a potential threat.

Emotion activates discomfort.

Avoidance reduces that discomfort.

Relief reinforces the avoidance.

Each cycle strengthens the pattern.

Over time, the loop begins influencing identity. Individuals may begin describing themselves in ways that reflect the pattern that has developed. Someone who repeatedly avoids difficult conversations may begin thinking of themselves as someone who "doesn't handle conflict well." Someone who consistently withdraws from uncertain opportunities may begin believing they are simply "not the kind of person who takes risks."

Identity gradually incorporates the pattern.

Once the narrative becomes part of the individual's sense of self, avoidance may begin appearing less like a choice and more like an inherent trait. The person may believe that their behavior reflects who they are rather than recognizing it as the result of a reinforcing loop within the system.

Meaning may also shift as the loop continues.

If avoidance consistently prevents individuals from pursuing experiences that once felt important, their sense of direction may begin narrowing. Goals that require emotional risk may appear less appealing. Activities that involve uncertainty may gradually disappear from daily life. Meaning becomes organized around maintaining safety rather than pursuing growth.

At this point the architecture of experience has reorganized itself around protection.

The emotional avoidance loop does not arise because individuals lack strength or motivation. It emerges because the psychological system is attempting to protect itself from discomfort using the tools available to it.

Avoidance provides quick relief, and the system naturally gravitates toward strategies that restore equilibrium.

Yet the long-term effect of the loop can be restrictive.

Because avoidance prevents the system from encountering experiences that might challenge the original interpretation, the mind never receives evidence that the feared situation may be manageable. Emotional responses remain intense because the system has not learned how to process them in the presence of the triggering experience.

The architecture becomes organized around preventing discomfort rather than integrating it.

Recognizing the emotional avoidance loop often represents the first step toward changing it. When individuals begin noticing how interpretation, emotion, identity, and meaning interact within this pattern, they can start examining the assumptions that sustain it.

Instead of immediately withdrawing from discomfort, they may begin exploring the interpretations that triggered the emotional response. They may notice how avoidance provides temporary relief while leaving the underlying interpretation untouched.

Through this awareness, the loop begins to loosen.

The goal is not to eliminate emotional discomfort from life. Such a goal would be impossible and undesirable. Emotions serve important regulatory functions within the architecture of experience. The goal instead is to allow the system to remain engaged with experience long enough for new interpretations and emotional responses to develop.

When individuals gradually replace avoidance with engagement, the architecture begins reorganizing itself. Interpretations become more flexible, emotional responses become more manageable, identity narratives expand, and meaning reconnects with values that encourage exploration rather than withdrawal.

In this way, understanding the emotional avoidance loop reveals how a simple pattern of relief can gradually shape the entire structure of psychological life.

The Identity Collapse Cycle

If the Emotional Avoidance Loop shows how the psychological system organizes itself around the reduction of discomfort, another structural pattern reveals how deeply the architecture of experience depends on the stability of identity. Human beings rely on identity to organize experience across time. It provides a narrative structure through which individuals understand who they are, what they value, and where they are going. When that narrative becomes unstable, the entire psychological system can enter a period of disorientation.

This dynamic is what Psychological Architecture describes as the Identity Collapse Cycle.

Identity is not simply a collection of personality traits or roles. It functions as an organizing framework that helps individuals interpret their experiences. When a person encounters success, failure, praise, criticism, or uncertainty, the mind interprets those experiences partly through the lens of identity. The narrative individuals hold about themselves shapes what those experiences appear to mean.

For example, someone who identifies strongly as competent may interpret a professional challenge as an opportunity to demonstrate skill. Someone who identifies strongly as responsible may interpret the same situation as an obligation to meet expectations. In both cases the identity narrative organizes interpretation and guides emotional response.

When identity remains flexible, it allows individuals to adapt to new experiences. Challenges become opportunities to expand the narrative rather than threats to its existence. Yet when identity becomes tightly connected to specific outcomes, roles, or assumptions about the self, it may become vulnerable to disruption.

The Identity Collapse Cycle often begins when an experience directly contradicts a central element of the identity narrative.

A person who sees themselves as dependable may suddenly encounter circumstances that make it impossible to fulfill an important commitment. Someone who identifies strongly with professional competence may experience repeated failure in a domain that once provided confidence. A parent who organizes identity around caregiving may face a moment when their child no longer needs the same level of involvement.

In these moments the individual is not merely confronting a difficult situation. The experience appears to challenge the story through which they understand who they are.

The interpretive engine of the mind quickly attempts to reconcile the discrepancy. It searches for explanations that preserve coherence within the narrative. Sometimes the mind concludes that the experience represents a temporary setback that does not fundamentally threaten the identity structure. When this interpretation succeeds, the system regains stability.

However, when the discrepancy becomes too large to ignore, emotional responses begin intensifying.

Shame, confusion, frustration, or grief may arise as the individual struggles to reconcile the experience with their identity narrative. These emotional responses signal that the architecture of the self is under strain. The system recognizes that the existing narrative may no longer fully explain what is happening.

At this stage individuals often attempt to protect the narrative.

They may reinterpret events in ways that preserve the identity structure. A professional setback may be attributed entirely to unfair circumstances. A relationship difficulty may be explained solely by the behavior of others. These interpretations help maintain coherence, but they may also prevent the system from integrating new information.

When these protective interpretations fail to resolve the tension, the cycle can intensify.

The individual may begin questioning not only the specific situation but the broader narrative that once defined their sense of self. Confidence that once felt stable may give way to uncertainty. The person may wonder whether the identity they have carried for years still reflects reality.

This questioning can feel deeply unsettling because identity functions as the organizing center of psychological experience. When the narrative weakens, interpretation becomes less certain, emotional responses become more volatile, and the sense of direction provided by meaning may begin to fade.

In this moment the system appears to be collapsing.

Yet the Identity Collapse Cycle does not necessarily end in permanent disintegration. In many cases the disruption marks the beginning of a restructuring process. When the existing narrative can no longer fully explain experience, the architecture of identity begins searching for a broader story that can integrate the new reality.

This search often involves revisiting earlier assumptions about the self.

Individuals may reconsider beliefs they once treated as permanent truths. They may begin distinguishing between roles they once held and the deeper values that guided them within those roles. Experiences that once appeared incompatible with the identity narrative may gradually be incorporated into a more complex understanding of the self.

Through this process the narrative expands.

A person who once defined themselves solely through professional success may begin integrating other dimensions of identity, such as relationships, creativity, or personal values. Someone who previously organized identity around a single role may discover new ways of understanding who they are beyond that role.

The collapse therefore becomes a transformation.

Instead of destroying the architecture of identity, the cycle exposes its limitations and invites the system to develop a more flexible structure. The individual's sense of self becomes less dependent on a narrow set of expectations and more capable of integrating diverse experiences.

From the perspective of Psychological Architecture, this process illustrates how identity remains both stable and evolving. It provides continuity across time, yet it must also remain capable of adapting as life unfolds.

Understanding the Identity Collapse Cycle helps individuals recognize that moments of profound self-doubt often signal an important structural transition within the architecture of experience. What appears to be a loss of identity may actually represent the beginning of a deeper and more resilient narrative.

The Self-Perception Map

If identity provides the narrative structure through which individuals understand who they are, another structural model helps explain how that narrative becomes reinforced through daily experience. Human beings are constantly observing themselves. They notice their own actions, reactions, successes, failures, and emotional responses. Over time these observations accumulate into a mental map that shapes how individuals see themselves.

Psychological Architecture describes this process through what can be called the Self-Perception Map.

The Self-Perception Map is not a single belief about oneself. Rather, it is an internal landscape composed of many smaller assumptions that gradually form through experience. These assumptions often begin as simple interpretations of specific events. A person who performs well in school may begin believing they are intellectually capable. Someone who struggles in social situations may begin believing they are awkward or uninteresting.

At first these interpretations remain tied to particular circumstances.

Yet as similar experiences repeat across time, the mind begins organizing them into broader conclusions about the self. The individual no longer sees the interpretation as a description of a single event. Instead, it becomes part of the mental map through which they understand who they are.

Once this map begins forming, it influences how the mind interprets future experiences.

Consider a student who has come to believe that they are "not good at mathematics." The belief may have originated from a few early struggles in school. However, once the interpretation becomes part of the self-perception map, it begins influencing how the student approaches future learning situations.

When a new mathematical problem appears, the mind may interpret the challenge as confirmation of the existing belief. Emotional responses such as anxiety or discouragement may arise quickly. These emotions influence attention and persistence, making it more difficult for the student to engage with the task effectively.

If the student then struggles with the problem, the experience reinforces the belief that they are not capable in that domain.

The self-perception map has begun organizing experience.

Importantly, the same dynamic can occur with positive assumptions about the self. A person who develops the belief that they are capable of learning new skills may approach unfamiliar situations with curiosity rather than fear. Emotional responses of interest and determination encourage exploration. Successful experiences then reinforce the belief that learning is possible.

In both cases the map influences perception.

What makes the Self-Perception Map particularly powerful is that it often operates beneath conscious awareness. Individuals rarely sit down and deliberately construct a theory about who they are. Instead, the map emerges gradually from repeated interpretations of experience.

Because the map feels familiar, individuals may treat it as an objective description of reality rather than as a set of interpretations that developed over time.

This is where the interaction between the four domains becomes especially important.

Interpretation contributes to the formation of the map by assigning meaning to events. Emotion amplifies certain experiences, making them more memorable. Identity organizes these experiences into a coherent narrative about the self. Meaning connects that narrative to broader values and life direction.

Together, these processes transform individual experiences into an internal geography through which future experiences are interpreted.

The map then begins guiding behavior.

Someone who sees themselves as capable may approach challenges with persistence. Someone who sees themselves as fragile may avoid situations that appear uncertain. These behaviors influence the experiences that follow. When individuals approach situations confidently, they often encounter opportunities that reinforce that confidence. When they withdraw from situations that feel threatening, they may never encounter the experiences that could revise their assumptions.

Over time the map appears increasingly accurate.

Yet the accuracy of the map often depends less on objective reality and more on the experiences individuals allow themselves to encounter. The map influences behavior, behavior influences experience, and experience reinforces the map.

This dynamic illustrates another important principle within Psychological Architecture. Human beings rarely perceive themselves in a neutral way. Instead, they observe themselves through interpretive frameworks that gradually shape the direction of their lives.

Recognizing the Self-Perception Map allows individuals to examine these frameworks more closely.

When people begin asking where particular beliefs about themselves originated, they often discover that those beliefs emerged from a limited set of experiences interpreted at a particular moment in time. What once appeared to be permanent truths may instead reflect interpretations that were never revisited.

This realization can create an opportunity for revision.

If the map was constructed through experience, it can also evolve through experience. When individuals allow themselves to engage with situations that challenge their assumptions, the architecture of interpretation, emotion, identity, and meaning begins integrating new information.

Gradually, the map changes.

The goal is not to replace one rigid self-description with another. Instead, the aim is to develop a more flexible map that allows individuals to see themselves as capable of growth, learning, and adaptation. A flexible map allows the architecture of experience to remain responsive to new information rather than confined by interpretations formed in the past.

Understanding the Self-Perception Map therefore reveals how deeply the narratives individuals carry about themselves influence the way they move through the world.

The Emotional Maturity Index

Human beings differ widely in the ways they respond to emotional pressure. Some individuals react quickly and intensely when confronted with frustration, criticism, or disappointment. Others appear able to remain steady in the presence of the same experiences, maintaining a sense of perspective even when circumstances become difficult. These differences are often described informally as differences in emotional maturity.

Within Psychological Architecture, emotional maturity can be understood as a structural capacity rather than a personality trait.

The Emotional Maturity Index describes how the psychological system responds when emotional activation rises. It reflects the degree to which the system can remain stable enough to integrate emotional experience rather than reacting immediately in an attempt to reduce discomfort.

To understand this model, it is helpful to return to the interaction between interpretation and emotion.

Every emotional response begins with interpretation. The mind encounters a situation and assigns meaning to it. If the interpretation suggests threat, injustice, rejection, or loss, the emotional system responds accordingly. Anger may appear when the mind interprets a situation as unfair. Anxiety may arise when the mind anticipates danger or uncertainty. Sadness may emerge when the mind perceives loss.

Once activated, emotion creates pressure within the system.

This pressure demands attention. Emotions evolved to signal situations that require response. Anger urges confrontation, anxiety urges preparation or avoidance, and sadness encourages withdrawal and reflection. These signals are not problems in themselves; they are part of the regulatory system that helps individuals respond to life.

The crucial difference lies in how the psychological system handles the activation.

In systems with lower emotional maturity, emotional activation quickly translates into reaction. The individual may respond immediately to reduce the discomfort produced by the emotion. Anger may lead to confrontation or harsh words. Anxiety may lead to avoidance or reassurance seeking. Shame may lead to defensiveness or withdrawal.

These reactions often provide temporary relief.

By expressing anger, escaping anxiety, or defending against shame, the individual reduces the emotional pressure within the system. Yet the underlying interpretation that triggered the emotion remains largely unexamined. Because the interpretation has not changed, similar emotional responses are likely to arise again when comparable situations occur.

The cycle continues.

In systems with higher emotional maturity, a different process unfolds. Emotional activation still occurs; maturity does not eliminate emotional experience. Instead, the system possesses enough internal stability to hold the emotional response without immediately translating it into action.

This pause creates space for reflection.

During this moment of stability, the interpretive engine of the mind can examine the situation more carefully. The individual may ask whether the initial interpretation fully captures what is happening. They may consider alternative explanations for the behavior of others or for the circumstances themselves.

Emotion remains present, but it no longer dictates the immediate response.

This capacity to remain present with emotional activation allows the architecture of experience to integrate the information contained within the emotion. Anger may reveal that a boundary has been crossed. Anxiety may signal genuine uncertainty that requires preparation. Sadness may reflect a loss that deserves acknowledgement.

Rather than reacting automatically, the individual can respond deliberately.

The Emotional Maturity Index therefore reflects the system's ability to maintain coherence when emotional pressure rises. A mature system does not avoid emotion, suppress it, or deny it. Instead, it allows emotion to exist within a broader context of interpretation, identity, and meaning.

Identity plays an important role in this process.

Individuals with higher emotional maturity often carry identity narratives that allow for complexity in emotional experience. They may see themselves as capable of handling discomfort without immediately resolving it. This narrative supports the system's ability to remain stable while emotions unfold.

Meaning also contributes to maturity.

When individuals connect emotional experiences to broader values or long-term purposes, they may tolerate temporary discomfort more easily. A difficult conversation may feel worthwhile when it aligns with values of honesty or responsibility. Anxiety about a challenging task may become manageable when the individual sees the effort as part of a meaningful goal.

In this way the Emotional Maturity Index reflects the integration of the entire architecture.

Interpretation becomes more flexible, allowing multiple perspectives on a situation. Emotion provides information without overwhelming the system. Identity supports resilience rather than defensiveness. Meaning connects the experience to values that extend beyond the immediate moment.

Importantly, emotional maturity is not fixed.

Individuals may demonstrate high maturity in some areas of life while struggling in others. A person who remains calm and reflective in professional settings may react quickly within family relationships where emotional histories are deeper. The architecture of experience contains many layers, and maturity can evolve over time.

Recognizing the Emotional Maturity Index allows individuals to observe how their system responds under pressure.

Instead of evaluating themselves harshly for emotional reactions, they can begin examining the structure of those reactions. They may notice when the system moves quickly toward relief and when it possesses enough stability to remain engaged with emotional experience.

Through this awareness, the capacity for maturity can gradually expand.

The goal is not emotional perfection. Human emotional life will always involve moments of reactivity, misunderstanding, and regret. The aim instead is to strengthen the architecture of the system so that emotional activation becomes an opportunity for integration rather than a trigger for automatic reaction.

Understanding the Emotional Maturity Index reveals how the architecture of experience determines whether emotional pressure leads to reaction or reflection.

Emotional Repatterning

The structural models described in this chapter reveal something important about human psychological life. Patterns within the architecture of experience do not arise randomly. They develop through repeated interactions among interpretation, emotion, identity, and meaning. Over time those interactions form loops and cycles that organize how individuals respond to the world.

Yet if patterns can form through repetition, they can also change through new experience.

This possibility introduces the final structural model within Psychological Architecture: Emotional Repatterning.

Emotional repatterning describes the process through which the architecture of experience gradually reorganizes itself when individuals begin engaging with emotional experiences in new ways. Unlike sudden moments of insight, repatterning is typically gradual. It unfolds through repeated experiences that introduce new interpretations, new emotional responses, and new identity narratives into the system.

To understand how repatterning occurs, it is useful to return to the role of emotional experience within the architecture.

Emotions provide signals about how the mind interprets situations. When individuals encounter circumstances that trigger strong emotional responses, the architecture is revealing something about the assumptions currently organizing the system. Anxiety may indicate that the mind anticipates danger. Anger may signal a perceived violation of expectations or boundaries. Shame may arise when the individual believes they have failed to meet important standards.

These emotional signals are not simply disturbances to eliminate. They are information.

When individuals attempt to remove emotional discomfort immediately through avoidance or reaction, the underlying interpretation that generated the emotion often remains unchanged. As we saw in the Emotional Avoidance Loop, this pattern can gradually organize the architecture around strategies designed primarily to reduce discomfort.

Repatterning begins when individuals allow themselves to remain present with emotional experience long enough for new interpretations to emerge.

This does not mean seeking out distress unnecessarily. Instead, it involves remaining engaged with experiences that naturally produce emotional activation rather than automatically withdrawing from them. When individuals stay present with these experiences, the architecture gains an opportunity to integrate new information.

Consider someone who has developed a pattern of avoiding difficult conversations. Each time the individual withdraws from the situation, the architecture reinforces the interpretation that such conversations are overwhelming or dangerous. The emotional system learns that avoidance provides relief, and the loop becomes stronger.

When the individual begins experimenting with engagement rather than withdrawal, something different becomes possible.

The first attempt may still produce anxiety. The emotional response does not disappear immediately simply because the individual has chosen to act differently. However, if the person remains present in the conversation long enough to experience a different outcome than expected, the architecture receives new information.

Perhaps the conversation leads to understanding rather than conflict. Perhaps the other person responds with openness rather than hostility. Even if the conversation remains difficult, the individual may discover that they are capable of navigating the experience without collapsing emotionally.

Each of these outcomes introduces a new interpretation.

Over time, repeated experiences like this begin altering the structure of the system. The mind gradually revises its expectations about what similar situations will produce. Emotional responses become less intense because the architecture no longer interprets the situation exclusively through the lens of threat.

Identity also begins evolving.

Instead of seeing themselves as someone who avoids conflict, the individual may begin integrating a new narrative about their capacity to handle difficult conversations. This narrative does not erase past experiences, but it expands the story the person tells about who they are.

Meaning shifts as well.

Experiences that once appeared threatening may begin to feel connected to values such as honesty, courage, or growth. The individual may recognize that engaging with difficult situations allows them to live more consistently with those values.

Through this process the architecture reorganizes itself.

Interpretation becomes more flexible. Emotional responses become more regulated. Identity narratives expand to include new capabilities. Meaning reconnects experience with deeper values. The pattern that once dominated the system gradually loses its influence.

Repatterning does not occur instantly.

The architecture of human experience develops over many years, and patterns formed through repetition rarely dissolve in a single moment. New experiences must accumulate before the system fully integrates alternative interpretations and responses. During this period individuals may notice that old reactions still appear occasionally, even as new responses begin emerging.

This fluctuation is part of the process.

Repatterning involves the gradual strengthening of new patterns rather than the sudden elimination of old ones. With each experience that introduces a different interpretation or emotional response, the architecture gains additional evidence that the system can function in new ways.

Over time the balance shifts.

What once felt automatic becomes optional. Situations that previously triggered avoidance or reactivity may begin producing curiosity or confidence instead. Identity narratives expand, and meaning becomes connected to a broader range of possibilities.

Through emotional repatterning, the architecture of experience reveals one of its most important qualities.

It is not a fixed structure.

Human beings carry within them a system capable of reorganizing itself in response to new understanding and experience. When individuals learn to engage with their emotional life in ways that allow interpretation, identity, and meaning to evolve, the architecture becomes increasingly capable of supporting growth.

The patterns that once defined psychological life become the foundation upon which new patterns can emerge.

* * *

8

Integration: Building a Coherent Psychological Structure

Change in human psychological life is often imagined as a dramatic moment. People speak of breakthroughs, turning points, or sudden realizations that appear to transform the direction of a life overnight. While such moments do occur, the deeper reality of psychological change is usually quieter and more gradual. The architecture of human experience rarely reorganizes itself in a single moment. Instead, change unfolds as the system slowly adjusts to new interpretations, emotional experiences, identity narratives, and sources of meaning.

To understand this process, it is important to remember that the patterns described in the previous chapter did not form suddenly. The Emotional Avoidance Loop, the Identity Collapse Cycle, the Self-Perception Map, and the dynamics of emotional maturity all emerge through repeated interactions within the architecture of experience. Interpretation, emotion, identity, and meaning continually influence one another, gradually organizing the system into stable patterns that shape how individuals experience the world.

Because these patterns develop through repetition, change also occurs through repetition.

When individuals begin engaging with their experiences in ways that introduce new interpretations or emotional responses, the architecture

122

gradually incorporates that new information. The process may feel slow at first because the system has already learned patterns that once helped maintain stability. Those patterns do not disappear immediately. Instead, the architecture begins experimenting with alternative ways of organizing experience.

The first step in this process often involves awareness.

Many psychological patterns operate beneath conscious attention. Individuals may notice the outcomes produced by these patterns—conflict in relationships, persistent anxiety, a sense of directionlessness—without clearly seeing the underlying dynamics that generate those outcomes. When the architecture becomes strained, however, those dynamics sometimes become more visible.

A person may begin noticing how quickly their mind interprets certain situations as threatening. They may recognize how emotional responses escalate before they have time to reflect on what is happening. They may observe how identity narratives influence their expectations about themselves and others.

This recognition does not immediately resolve the pattern, but it introduces a crucial shift within the system.

When individuals can observe the architecture of their experience rather than simply reacting within it, a new form of psychological space emerges. The interpretive engine of the mind begins examining its own assumptions. Emotional responses can be noticed without immediately determining behavior. Identity narratives can be questioned rather than automatically defended.

Awareness allows the system to pause.

In that pause, the architecture becomes capable of integrating new possibilities. Instead of repeating the same interpretive pattern automatically, the individual may begin considering alternative perspectives. Instead of responding immediately to emotional pressure, the system may remain stable long enough to examine the emotion more carefully.

These moments of awareness may appear small, but they represent the beginning of structural change.

Each time the architecture remains open to new interpretations or emotional experiences, it gathers evidence that the system can function differently than it did before. Over time, these experiences accumulate. The mind becomes more flexible in its interpretations. Emotional responses become easier to regulate. Identity narratives expand to include new dimensions of experience.

Meaning begins shifting as well.

Experiences that once appeared confusing or discouraging may begin to feel connected to growth or learning. Challenges that once seemed like threats to identity may become opportunities to revise the narrative through which the individual understands their life.

This gradual reorganization illustrates an important principle of Psychological Architecture: change occurs not by removing parts of the system but by integrating them more effectively.

Interpretation remains necessary because human beings must constantly make sense of experience. Emotion remains essential because it signals what matters and motivates action. Identity continues organizing the narrative of the self, and meaning continues connecting experience to values and direction.

The difference lies in how these domains interact.

When the architecture becomes more integrated, interpretation becomes less rigid, emotional responses become more informative than overwhelming, identity becomes more flexible, and meaning becomes connected to values that can adapt to changing circumstances.

Psychological change therefore involves strengthening the system's ability to integrate experience.

Rather than reacting to emotional signals with avoidance or defensiveness, the architecture gradually learns to remain present with those signals long enough for new understanding to emerge. Instead of protecting a fixed narrative about the self, identity becomes capable of incorporating new experiences without collapsing.

Through this process the system becomes more resilient.

Resilience in this sense does not mean the absence of difficulty. Human life will always involve uncertainty, disappointment, and loss. What changes is the architecture's ability to absorb those experiences without becoming trapped in patterns that restrict growth.

As individuals become more aware of the structure of their psychological life, they begin participating more consciously in its evolution. The architecture that once organized experience automatically becomes a system they can observe, understand, and gradually reshape through the choices they make and the interpretations they adopt.

The following sections explore how this reorganization unfolds within the different domains of Psychological Architecture, revealing how awareness and engagement gradually transform the patterns that shape human experience.

Awareness as the First Structural Shift

When psychological patterns begin changing, the shift rarely begins with behavior alone. Behavior may appear to be the most visible aspect of change, but deeper transformation usually starts earlier in the architecture of experience. The first structural shift often occurs in awareness.

Awareness allows individuals to see the patterns operating within their psychological system.

For much of life, interpretation, emotion, identity, and meaning interact automatically. The mind interprets events quickly, emotional responses follow those interpretations, identity organizes the experience into the ongoing narrative of the self, and meaning connects the experience to broader values or expectations about life. Because these processes occur rapidly and continuously, individuals often experience them as simple reality rather than as the activity of an internal system.

Awareness interrupts this assumption.

When individuals begin noticing how their interpretations form, how their emotions activate, and how their identity narratives influence their responses, the architecture of experience becomes visible in a new way. What once appeared to be an unavoidable reaction may begin to look like a pattern within the system.

For example, someone might notice that certain situations repeatedly produce anxiety. In the past, the anxiety may have felt like an inevitable response to external circumstances. Through awareness, the individual may begin observing how quickly the mind interprets those situations as threatening. They may notice the sequence through which interpretation activates emotion, and how the emotional response influences their behavior.

This observation creates distance within the system.

Instead of being fully absorbed within the reaction, the individual becomes capable of examining it. The mind begins observing its own interpretive patterns. Emotional activation can be recognized without immediately dictating action. Identity narratives that once felt unquestionable may begin to appear as stories the individual has carried about themselves.

This shift is subtle but powerful.

Awareness does not immediately dissolve emotional responses or remove the interpretations that produced them. Anxiety may still arise when uncertainty appears. Anger may still activate when a boundary feels violated. Yet awareness changes how the system relates to these experiences.

When awareness is present, the emotional response becomes information rather than instruction.

Instead of reacting automatically, the individual may begin asking what interpretation produced the emotion. They may explore whether alternative explanations are possible. They may notice how their identity narrative influences the way they interpret the situation.

Through this process the architecture becomes more flexible.

Interpretation begins expanding beyond a single automatic assumption. Emotional responses remain present but no longer dictate behavior as strongly as before. Identity narratives begin accommodating more complex experiences, and meaning becomes less tied to rigid expectations about how life must unfold.

Awareness also reveals how patterns repeat across different areas of life.

A person who becomes attentive to their reactions may begin noticing similar interpretive patterns appearing in different contexts. The same expectation of criticism may appear in professional situations and personal relationships. The same impulse toward avoidance may arise in different forms whenever emotional discomfort appears.

Recognizing these repetitions allows individuals to see the structural nature of the pattern.

What once felt like separate problems may reveal themselves as expressions of a single dynamic within the architecture of experience. This recognition is often the moment when individuals begin understanding how their psychological system organizes itself.

From this perspective, awareness becomes the foundation of change.

Without awareness, the architecture continues repeating familiar patterns because the system remains unaware that those patterns exist. With awareness, the interpretive engine of the mind gains the ability to question its own assumptions. Emotional responses can be held within a broader context rather than immediately acted upon.

Identity narratives may begin evolving as individuals realize that their past interpretations do not fully determine who they are capable of becoming.

Meaning also shifts in response to awareness.

Experiences that once appeared confusing or discouraging may begin to feel connected to a larger process of learning and development. The individual may see that the architecture of experience is not simply something that happens to them. It is a system through which they participate in shaping the direction of their lives.

Awareness therefore represents the first structural shift in psychological change.

It transforms the architecture from an automatic system into one that can be observed and gradually reorganized. Each moment of awareness introduces the possibility of responding differently than before.

Through this process, the patterns that once defined psychological life begin slowly loosening their hold on the system.

Interrupting Psychological Loops

Once individuals become aware of the patterns shaping their psychological experience, the next stage of change involves learning how those patterns can be interrupted. Awareness reveals the structure of a loop, but interruption alters the direction in which the loop moves.

Psychological loops form when the same interaction among interpretation, emotion, identity, and behavior repeats often enough to become self-reinforcing. As described earlier in the Emotional Avoidance Loop and the Identity Collapse Cycle, the system begins expecting certain outcomes, and those expectations guide perception and behavior in ways that confirm the pattern.

Interrupting these loops does not require eliminating emotional responses or forcing the mind to think differently immediately. Instead, interruption occurs when a single element within the pattern begins responding differently than it did before.

Consider again the structure of a reinforcing loop.

An interpretation forms about a situation.

That interpretation produces an emotional response.

The emotion encourages a particular action.

The outcome of that action reinforces the interpretation.

When this sequence repeats many times, the pattern begins appearing inevitable. Individuals may feel as though their responses are simply dictated by circumstances rather than shaped by the structure of the system.

Interruption begins when one step in the sequence changes.

For example, someone who typically withdraws from situations that produce anxiety may experiment with remaining present slightly longer than usual. The emotional response may still arise, but the behavioral response changes. By staying engaged rather than withdrawing, the individual creates the possibility of a different outcome.

The mind then receives new information.

If the feared outcome does not occur, the interpretation that triggered the anxiety may begin weakening. Even if the situation remains uncomfortable, the individual may discover that the emotional response is tolerable rather than overwhelming. Each experience like this introduces a small shift within the loop.

Over time, these shifts accumulate.

Another form of interruption occurs at the level of interpretation. Instead of accepting the first explanation that arises, individuals may begin exploring alternative interpretations of a situation. A delayed response from a friend might initially be interpreted as rejection. With greater awareness, the individual may consider other explanations such as distraction, fatigue, or misunderstanding.

This interpretive flexibility can soften emotional responses before they intensify.

Emotion itself can also become the point of interruption. When individuals recognize emotional activation early, they may begin responding to the emotion with curiosity rather than immediate action. Instead of reacting to anger or anxiety automatically, the individual allows the emotion to exist without translating it immediately into behavior.

This pause changes the rhythm of the system.

The loop no longer moves at the same speed. The interpretive engine has time to examine its assumptions. Emotional intensity may rise and fall naturally rather than escalating through reactive behavior.

Identity narratives may also evolve during this process.

Individuals who once saw themselves as trapped within certain patterns may begin recognizing their capacity to respond differently. Each successful interruption of a loop introduces evidence that the identity narrative can expand beyond the assumptions that previously defined it.

Meaning gradually shifts as well.

Experiences that once appeared to confirm limitations may begin appearing as opportunities to practice new responses. Instead of interpreting emotional discomfort as a signal to withdraw, individuals may begin seeing it as an invitation to explore the architecture of their experience more deeply.

This shift transforms the role of difficulty within psychological life.

Rather than serving only as a source of distress, challenging experiences become moments where the architecture of interpretation, emotion, identity, and meaning can reorganize itself.

Interrupting psychological loops therefore does not require dramatic change.

Often the process begins with small adjustments repeated across time. A brief pause before responding to an emotional trigger. A willingness to question an automatic interpretation. A decision to remain present in a situation that once would have been avoided.

Each interruption alters the pattern slightly.

Over time the system begins recognizing that the familiar loop is not the only possible way of organizing experience. New interactions among interpretation, emotion, identity, and meaning begin forming. The architecture of psychological life gradually reorganizes itself around these emerging patterns.

Through repeated interruption and experimentation, individuals discover that the patterns governing their experience are not permanent structures but dynamic processes capable of evolving.

Reorganizing Identity

As psychological patterns begin shifting through awareness and the interruption of reinforcing loops, another deeper transformation often unfolds within the architecture of experience. The narrative individuals hold about who they are begins to reorganize.

Identity, as we have seen, functions as the organizing story of the self. It provides continuity across time by connecting past experiences, present actions, and expectations about the future. When identity remains rigid, the psychological system may resist experiences that do not fit the existing narrative. When identity becomes flexible, however, the architecture gains the ability to integrate new information without destabilizing the entire system.

Reorganizing identity is therefore a central element of psychological change.

This process often begins when individuals notice that their existing narrative no longer fully explains their experiences. A person who has long seen themselves as incapable of handling conflict may begin discovering that they are able to navigate difficult conversations more effectively than they once believed. Someone who once defined themselves through a particular professional role may find that their interests and values have evolved in ways that extend beyond that role.

These experiences introduce tension within the identity narrative.

At first the mind may attempt to interpret the new experiences as exceptions rather than as evidence that the narrative itself might need revision. The system often prefers preserving coherence because the identity story provides stability. Yet as new experiences accumulate, the discrepancy between the narrative and reality becomes more difficult to ignore.

Gradually the individual begins reconsidering the assumptions that once defined the self.

This reconsideration does not require abandoning the past. Instead, the architecture of identity begins integrating earlier experiences into a broader narrative. What once appeared to be defining limitations may be reinterpreted as temporary stages of development. Events that once felt like failures may begin appearing as turning points that shaped later understanding.

Through this process the narrative expands.

A person who once saw themselves as socially withdrawn may begin integrating experiences of meaningful connection into their identity story. Someone who once believed they lacked resilience may begin recognizing moments in their past where they endured difficulty and continued forward.

These recognitions do not erase earlier struggles.

Instead, they place those struggles within a larger narrative that includes growth, adaptation, and learning. The identity structure becomes less dependent on a narrow set of experiences and more capable of incorporating the complexity of life.

Reorganizing identity also influences interpretation and emotion.

When individuals carry a broader narrative about who they are, the interpretive engine of the mind becomes more flexible. Situations that once appeared threatening to identity may begin appearing as opportunities to express different aspects of the self. Emotional responses may become less defensive because the architecture no longer treats every challenge as a threat to the narrative.

Meaning evolves alongside this process.

Values that once appeared tied to a specific role or outcome may begin connecting to deeper principles that remain stable across changing circumstances. Someone who once derived meaning primarily from professional achievement may begin discovering meaning in relationships, creativity, or contribution to others.

As meaning expands, the identity narrative becomes more resilient.

Instead of relying on a single source of validation, the architecture of the self begins drawing stability from multiple dimensions of experience. This diversification allows individuals to encounter setbacks without feeling that their entire sense of identity has collapsed.

Importantly, reorganizing identity does not require constructing an entirely new story about the self.

Human identity develops across a lifetime of experiences, relationships, and values. The process of reorganization involves weaving those elements together in ways that reflect both continuity and change. The narrative evolves while remaining connected to the individual's history.

Through this integration, identity becomes less rigid and more dynamic.

Individuals begin seeing themselves not as fixed characters within a predetermined story, but as participants in an evolving narrative that continues unfolding over time. This perspective allows the architecture of experience to remain open to new interpretations, emotional responses, and possibilities for meaning.

The reorganization of identity therefore marks a profound stage in psychological change.

When individuals revise the story through which they understand themselves, the entire architecture of experience becomes capable of supporting new patterns of life.

Restoring Meaning

As psychological change unfolds, the reorganization of identity often leads naturally to another transformation within the architecture of experience: the restoration of meaning. Meaning functions as the integrative domain that connects interpretation, emotion, and identity to a sense of direction. When meaning weakens, individuals may feel as though their lives have lost coherence or purpose. When meaning becomes reestablished, the architecture regains a sense of orientation.

Periods of psychological difficulty often involve a disruption of meaning.

When individuals encounter repeated setbacks, identity challenges, or emotional strain, the activities and goals that once provided direction may begin to feel disconnected from their deeper values. A career path that once appeared fulfilling may begin to feel empty. Relationships that once felt stable may appear uncertain. The narrative through which individuals understood their life may no longer provide the same sense of purpose.

During such periods, individuals often experience a form of existential questioning.

They may begin asking themselves whether the path they have followed truly reflects what matters most to them. They may question whether the goals they once pursued were shaped by external expectations rather than by their own values. The loss of meaning can create a sense of disorientation because the architecture of experience depends on meaning to organize the direction of effort.

Yet this disruption also creates the possibility of rediscovery.

When individuals step back from the goals or roles that once defined their sense of purpose, they gain the opportunity to examine the values that remain important beneath those roles. A person who once derived meaning primarily from professional achievement may rediscover values related to learning, contribution, creativity, or connection with others.

These values provide the foundation for rebuilding meaning.

Meaning does not arise automatically from external circumstances. Instead, it emerges when individuals connect their actions and experiences to values they recognize as significant. The architecture of experience becomes oriented toward those values, allowing individuals to see how their daily choices contribute to something that matters to them.

This orientation changes how challenges are interpreted.

Difficult experiences that once appeared meaningless may begin to feel connected to growth, responsibility, or commitment to something larger than immediate comfort. Effort that once seemed burdensome may begin to feel worthwhile when it aligns with deeply held values.

Emotion responds to this shift as well.

When individuals reconnect with meaningful goals, emotional responses often become more balanced. Anxiety may still arise when facing uncertainty, but it becomes part of a purposeful effort rather than a signal of hopelessness. Frustration may occur when obstacles appear, yet it exists within the context of pursuing something that remains important.

Identity integrates this new orientation.

The narrative individuals carry about themselves begins incorporating the values that now guide their choices. Instead of defining identity primarily through past roles or expectations, the individual begins seeing themselves as someone who acts in accordance with values that provide direction.

Meaning therefore strengthens the architecture of experience.

Interpretation becomes guided by values rather than by fear alone. Emotional responses become connected to purposeful effort rather than to avoidance. Identity becomes organized around principles that can endure even as circumstances change.

Importantly, restoring meaning does not require discovering a single grand purpose that defines the entire course of a life.

Meaning often arises from multiple sources. Relationships, creative expression, learning, service to others, and the pursuit of personal growth can all provide direction. What matters is that these sources of meaning connect experience to values that individuals recognize as genuinely important.

When this connection becomes clear, the architecture of experience regains coherence.

Life once again appears oriented toward something rather than simply reacting to circumstances. The psychological system begins integrating interpretation, emotion, identity, and action around values that guide the individual forward.

Through the restoration of meaning, the architecture of human experience becomes capable of supporting a renewed sense of direction.

Psychological Growth as Structural Integration

When the architecture of experience reorganizes successfully, the result is not simply the absence of distress. Psychological growth does not mean that emotional discomfort disappears or that life becomes permanently stable. Instead, growth reflects a deeper integration of the domains that shape human experience.

Interpretation becomes more flexible, emotion becomes more informative rather than overwhelming, identity becomes more expansive, and meaning becomes more deeply connected to values that can endure across changing circumstances. The architecture remains the same, but the relationships among its domains become more balanced.

This integration allows individuals to move through life with greater psychological stability.

Challenges continue to appear, as they do in every human life. Situations may still trigger uncertainty, frustration, disappointment, or grief. Yet the system becomes better able to absorb these experiences without collapsing into rigid patterns of avoidance, defensiveness, or confusion.

Interpretation begins adapting more easily to new information.

Instead of relying on a single explanation for events, the mind becomes capable of considering multiple perspectives. Situations that once triggered immediate assumptions may now invite curiosity or reflection. This flexibility allows individuals to respond more accurately to the complexity of real life.

Emotion also becomes more integrated within the system.

Rather than reacting automatically to emotional signals, individuals develop the capacity to experience emotion without becoming overwhelmed by it. Anger can reveal the need to address a boundary. Anxiety can signal uncertainty that requires preparation. Sadness can acknowledge loss without eliminating hope for the future.

Emotion becomes part of the information the architecture uses to guide action.

Identity undergoes a similar transformation.

When identity becomes more integrated, individuals no longer rely on a narrow narrative about who they must be. The story of the self expands to include multiple dimensions of experience. A person may see themselves as capable of strength and vulnerability, confidence and uncertainty, achievement and learning.

This broader narrative allows identity to remain stable even when circumstances change.

Meaning becomes the element that connects these changes to the direction of life.

When individuals organize their actions around values rather than rigid expectations, they become capable of pursuing goals while adapting to the realities they encounter along the way. Meaning provides orientation without requiring that every outcome unfold exactly as imagined.

The architecture therefore becomes resilient.

Resilience in this context does not refer to toughness or emotional suppression. It reflects the system's ability to remain coherent when confronted with difficulty. Interpretation can adjust, emotion can be experienced and processed, identity can adapt, and meaning can continue guiding the individual forward.

Growth also changes how individuals relate to their own psychological patterns.

Instead of viewing past patterns with shame or frustration, individuals often begin seeing them as part of the system's earlier attempts to maintain stability. Avoidance, defensiveness, or confusion may once have been the best strategies available to the architecture at the time.

With new awareness and experience, the system learns new strategies.

This perspective allows individuals to approach their psychological history with greater understanding. Past struggles become sources of insight rather than evidence of personal failure. The architecture of experience becomes something to learn from rather than something to criticize.

Over time, this integration creates a deeper sense of coherence within the system.

Individuals may feel more capable of navigating uncertainty because they trust the architecture of their experience to adapt. Emotional responses become less frightening because they are understood as signals rather than threats. Identity becomes a narrative that continues evolving rather than a fixed definition that must be defended.

Meaning provides a stable orientation through all of these changes.

Life remains unpredictable, but the architecture of experience becomes capable of responding to that unpredictability with flexibility and intention. Individuals begin recognizing that the structure of their psychological life is not something imposed upon them from outside. It is a system that evolves through their interpretations, their emotional engagement with experience, the stories they tell about themselves, and the values that guide their actions.

Psychological growth, from the perspective of Psychological Architecture, is therefore not the construction of a perfect life.

It is the gradual integration of the system that allows individuals to live more consciously within the architecture of their own experience.

* * *

9

Living Within the Architecture

By the time individuals begin understanding the structure of their psychological life, something subtle but significant changes in how they experience the world. The events of life do not suddenly become easier, nor do emotional responses disappear. Challenges still arise, relationships remain complex, and uncertainty continues to shape the course of human experience. Yet the way individuals relate to these experiences begins to shift.

They are no longer encountering life without a framework for understanding what is happening within them.

Throughout this book we have explored the architecture through which human experience unfolds. The mind interprets events and attempts to organize the world into patterns of meaning. Emotion responds to those interpretations, signaling what matters and motivating action. Identity gathers experiences into the narrative through which individuals understand who they are across time. Meaning integrates those narratives with values and direction, allowing life to feel oriented toward something larger than the moment itself.

These domains are always operating.

Whether individuals recognize them or not, interpretation, emotion, identity, and meaning interact continuously to shape the structure of psychological life. For much of human history, people have experienced these dynamics without clearly understanding how they function together. Reactions feel immediate, emotions appear mysterious, and identity narratives seem to define the self in ways that are difficult to question.

Understanding the architecture changes this relationship.

When individuals begin seeing how these domains interact, their psychological experiences become more intelligible. Instead of feeling as though their reactions emerge from nowhere, they can begin recognizing the processes that give rise to those reactions. Interpretation can be examined. Emotional responses can be understood as signals rather than problems. Identity narratives can be explored and revised. Meaning can be rediscovered when life begins to feel directionless.

This understanding does not remove difficulty from life.

Human beings will always encounter disappointment, uncertainty, loss, and conflict. These experiences are not flaws in the architecture of psychological life; they are part of the conditions within which human lives unfold. The value of understanding the architecture lies not in eliminating these experiences but in recognizing how the system responds to them.

When individuals see the architecture clearly, they gain a different relationship with their own psychological processes.

Instead of becoming trapped within patterns of reaction, they may begin observing those patterns with curiosity. They can notice how certain interpretations generate emotional responses, how identity narratives influence expectations, and how meaning shapes the direction of effort. This awareness creates space within the system.

In that space, choice becomes possible.

Choice does not mean that individuals can control every emotional response or every interpretation that arises in the mind. Much of psychological life remains automatic because the architecture is designed to respond quickly to experience. Yet awareness allows individuals to participate more consciously in how those responses evolve.

They can examine interpretations that once appeared unquestionable. They can remain present with emotions that once triggered immediate reaction. They can revise the narratives through which they understand themselves. They can reconnect their lives with values that provide direction even when circumstances remain uncertain.

Living within the architecture therefore means learning to inhabit the system with greater understanding.

The domains of mind, emotion, identity, and meaning continue interacting as they always have. What changes is the clarity with which individuals recognize those interactions. Psychological life becomes less mysterious and more navigable.

This clarity also brings a new form of humility.

When individuals recognize the complexity of the architecture shaping their experience, they often become more patient with themselves and with others. Emotional reactions that once seemed irrational begin to appear as understandable responses within a larger system. Conflicts that once appeared purely personal may reveal deeper patterns within the architecture of human interaction.

Understanding the system does not remove responsibility, but it does deepen compassion.

People are no longer viewed simply as collections of behaviors or traits. They are understood as individuals navigating the architecture of interpretation, emotion, identity, and meaning, often without having been given the tools to recognize how those domains interact.

With that recognition, psychological understanding becomes less about judging behavior and more about understanding the structure from which behavior emerges.

Living within the architecture of human experience therefore invites a different relationship with oneself and with the world. Instead of searching for perfect control over emotions or circumstances, individuals begin developing a deeper familiarity with the system through which they experience life.

And through that familiarity, the architecture that once operated invisibly becomes something that can be understood, respected, and gradually shaped through awareness and engagement.

The Ongoing Nature of Psychological Life

Understanding the architecture of human experience does not mark the end of psychological development. If anything, it reveals that psychological life is an ongoing process rather than a problem to be solved once and for all. Interpretation continues adjusting to new circumstances, emotions continue responding to those interpretations, identity continues evolving across time, and meaning continues shifting as individuals encounter new values and responsibilities.

In this sense, psychological life is never finished.

The architecture described throughout this book does not produce a final state of stability in which interpretation becomes permanently accurate, emotions remain perfectly regulated, identity remains completely secure, and meaning remains fixed. Human life unfolds in changing environments, through relationships that grow and transform, and through experiences that introduce new challenges and opportunities.

Because life continues changing, the architecture of experience must remain dynamic.

Individuals who understand this reality often discover that psychological growth becomes less about achieving a particular state and more about maintaining a relationship with the system itself. They begin paying attention to how their interpretations evolve as they encounter new situations. They observe how emotional responses shift across different stages of life. They notice how identity narratives expand as new roles and experiences emerge.

Meaning, too, continues developing.

Values that once guided a person's choices during early adulthood may be reexamined later in life as priorities shift. Responsibilities to family, community, or personal aspirations may gradually reshape how individuals understand what matters most to them. Meaning is not static; it evolves as the architecture integrates new experiences.

This ongoing nature of psychological life can feel unsettling at first.

Many people hope that personal development will eventually lead to a permanent state of certainty or emotional equilibrium. When individuals encounter new challenges even after significant growth, they may wonder whether they have somehow failed to maintain the stability they once achieved.

Yet from the perspective of Psychological Architecture, these moments are not signs of failure.

They reflect the normal functioning of a system that must continually adapt to new circumstances. As life unfolds, interpretation encounters unfamiliar situations, emotional responses arise in new contexts, identity incorporates additional experiences, and meaning adjusts to reflect changing values.

The architecture is doing exactly what it was designed to do.

Understanding this dynamic allows individuals to approach their psychological life with greater patience. Instead of expecting themselves to respond perfectly to every situation, they can recognize that each new experience represents another opportunity for the architecture to integrate information and evolve.

This perspective also encourages curiosity.

When individuals encounter emotional reactions or interpretive patterns that surprise them, they may begin exploring what those responses reveal about the system. Rather than judging themselves for experiencing uncertainty or discomfort, they can ask how the architecture is attempting to interpret and regulate the situation.

Through this curiosity, psychological life becomes an ongoing conversation with the self.

Interpretation learns from experience. Emotion provides information about what matters. Identity adapts to incorporate new dimensions of the individual's life. Meaning continues connecting those experiences to values that provide direction.

Living within the architecture therefore involves recognizing that the system will continue evolving throughout a lifetime.

Moments of stability will alternate with periods of questioning. Confidence will coexist with uncertainty. Growth will occur alongside moments of difficulty. These fluctuations are not evidence that the architecture has failed but signs that it remains responsive to the complexity of human life.

Over time, individuals who understand this ongoing process often develop a deeper sense of trust in their psychological system.

They recognize that the architecture is capable of absorbing new experiences and reorganizing itself when necessary. Even when life becomes uncertain, the system retains the capacity to interpret, regulate, integrate, and orient experience toward meaning.

The journey of psychological life therefore continues as long as life itself unfolds.

Living with Awareness of the System

When individuals begin understanding the architecture of their psychological life, awareness gradually becomes part of their daily experience. This awareness does not mean that every thought, emotion, or interpretation must be examined constantly. Human life would become exhausting if every internal process required deliberate analysis. Instead, awareness functions more like a background understanding of how the system operates.

People begin recognizing the patterns that once seemed invisible.

They may notice how quickly the mind interprets ambiguous situations according to familiar expectations. They may observe emotional responses rising and falling in ways that reflect those interpretations. They may become more attentive to the narratives through which they understand themselves and the values that shape the direction of their choices.

This awareness changes how individuals relate to their experiences.

Situations that once triggered immediate reactions may now invite reflection. An emotional response can be noticed without immediately determining behavior. Identity narratives that once appeared unquestionable may be explored with curiosity rather than defended automatically.

Living with awareness of the system therefore introduces a different rhythm into psychological life.

The architecture continues functioning as it always has, yet individuals develop the capacity to pause within the process. That pause allows interpretation to expand beyond its first assumption. Emotional responses can be experienced without instantly requiring resolution. Identity narratives can be examined in light of new experiences rather than preserved unchanged.

In practical terms, this awareness often appears in small moments.

A person may notice themselves preparing to withdraw from a difficult conversation and pause long enough to reconsider their interpretation of the situation. Someone experiencing frustration may recognize that their emotional response reflects a particular expectation rather than an objective reality. Another individual may realize that the story they have carried about themselves no longer fully reflects the person they have become.

These moments of recognition do not eliminate emotional responses or uncertainty.

Instead, they allow individuals to remain engaged with experience while the architecture processes what is happening. The system becomes capable of integrating information rather than reacting automatically to reduce discomfort.

Awareness also changes how individuals understand the behavior of others.

When people recognize how interpretation, emotion, identity, and meaning interact within their own experience, they often begin seeing these dynamics in the lives of others as well. Emotional reactions that once appeared irrational may become more understandable when viewed as part of a larger psychological pattern.

Conflicts may begin to appear less mysterious.

A disagreement between two people may involve different interpretations of the same situation, each shaped by the identity narratives and emotional histories they carry. Understanding this does not eliminate disagreement, but it can reduce the sense that the other person's reaction is inexplicable or malicious.

Awareness therefore contributes not only to personal growth but also to greater empathy.

Recognizing the architecture of human experience reveals how much of psychological life unfolds beneath the surface of conscious intention. People often react in ways that reflect patterns developed over many years rather than deliberate choices made in the moment.

When individuals see this more clearly, they may approach themselves and others with greater patience.

Living with awareness of the system also encourages a more thoughtful relationship with one's own values. Because meaning plays such an important role in organizing the architecture of experience, individuals who understand the system often become more attentive to the values guiding their choices.

They may begin asking whether their daily actions reflect what truly matters to them. They may reconsider goals that once appeared important but no longer align with their evolving understanding of meaning. This reflection helps maintain coherence within the architecture as life circumstances continue changing.

Over time, awareness becomes less like an effort and more like a form of familiarity.

Individuals become accustomed to recognizing how their interpretations, emotions, identity narratives, and values interact. Psychological life no longer feels like a series of unpredictable reactions but like a system whose dynamics they understand.

This familiarity does not grant control over every aspect of experience.

Instead, it provides orientation. Even when situations become difficult or uncertain, individuals can recognize the processes unfolding within them. They understand that interpretation is attempting to make sense of events, emotion is signaling what matters, identity is organizing the narrative of the self, and meaning is seeking direction.

With that understanding, living within the architecture becomes less about controlling life and more about participating consciously in the system through which life is experienced.

Responsibility and Psychological Agency

As individuals become more aware of the architecture shaping their experience, another dimension of psychological life begins to emerge more clearly: responsibility. This responsibility does not mean that individuals control every circumstance they encounter. Life continually introduces events that lie far beyond anyone's influence. Relationships change, opportunities appear or disappear, and unexpected challenges arise without warning.

Yet even within these changing conditions, individuals remain participants in the architecture through which those experiences are interpreted and integrated.

Psychological agency refers to this participation.

Agency does not mean absolute control over thoughts or emotions. Much of the architecture operates automatically because it evolved to respond quickly to the environment. Interpretations arise rapidly, emotions follow those interpretations, and identity narratives influence how individuals understand what is happening.

However, when awareness develops, individuals gain the ability to engage with these processes rather than simply being carried by them.

This engagement introduces a form of responsibility that is quieter but more significant than simple behavioral control. Individuals become responsible for how they examine their interpretations, how they respond to emotional signals, and how they shape the narratives through which they understand themselves.

For example, when an emotional response arises, individuals may not have chosen the emotion itself. Anger, anxiety, or sadness often appears before conscious reflection begins. Yet individuals can decide how they will respond to that emotional signal.

They can pause long enough to ask what interpretation produced the response. They can explore whether alternative interpretations might also be possible. They can decide whether their reaction will reinforce an existing pattern or introduce a different response within the architecture.

This is where psychological agency becomes visible.

Instead of reacting automatically to every emotional signal, individuals participate in shaping the direction of the system. Interpretation becomes something that can be examined. Emotional responses become signals that can inform action rather than dictate it.

Identity also becomes an area where agency emerges.

Many people carry narratives about themselves that developed earlier in life, often through experiences that were never carefully reconsidered. A person may believe they are incapable of leadership because of a few early failures. Another may believe they must always meet the expectations of others in order to maintain approval.

When individuals begin examining these narratives, they may discover that the stories they have carried about themselves are only partial descriptions of their experience. Through new experiences and reflection, they gain the ability to expand the narrative.

They begin shaping identity more consciously.

Meaning likewise becomes an area of responsibility.

Values that once guided an individual's life may have been inherited from family expectations, cultural assumptions, or social pressure. As awareness grows, individuals often begin examining whether those values truly reflect what matters most to them.

Choosing values is one of the most significant expressions of psychological agency.

When individuals decide which values will guide their actions, they influence how the architecture of their experience organizes itself. Interpretation begins aligning with those values, emotional responses become connected to their pursuit, identity incorporates them into the narrative of the self, and meaning provides direction through the challenges of life.

Responsibility within Psychological Architecture therefore does not involve controlling every outcome.

Instead, it involves participating consciously in the processes through which experience is interpreted, regulated, and integrated. Individuals recognize that their psychological life is not simply something that happens to them but something in which they actively take part.

This recognition can feel empowering, but it also requires humility.

Because the architecture of experience develops over time, individuals will inevitably encounter moments when old patterns reappear. Emotional reactions may emerge more quickly than reflection allows. Interpretations shaped by past experiences may influence perception before awareness has time to intervene.

These moments do not eliminate agency.

They simply remind individuals that psychological growth unfolds gradually. Responsibility lies not in achieving perfect control but in continuing to engage with the architecture of experience as it evolves.

Through this engagement, individuals begin shaping the direction of their psychological life.

Interpretation becomes more thoughtful. Emotional responses become more integrated. Identity narratives become more expansive. Meaning becomes connected to values that provide direction even when circumstances remain uncertain.

In this way, responsibility and agency become essential elements of living within the architecture of human experience.

The Architecture Across a Lifetime

The architecture of human experience does not appear suddenly at a single moment in life. It develops gradually as individuals move through different stages of growth, relationships, responsibilities, and changing circumstances. Interpretation, emotion, identity, and meaning begin interacting early in life and continue evolving across decades of experience.

Understanding the architecture therefore invites a broader perspective on how psychological life unfolds over time.

In early childhood, the architecture begins forming through simple interpretations of experience. A child learns how certain situations produce comfort while others create distress. Emotional responses become associated with particular interactions, and the earliest elements of identity begin emerging as the child interprets how others respond to them.

Meaning at this stage is relatively simple.

The child's sense of direction often revolves around safety, attachment, and belonging. Experiences that reinforce these needs become integrated into the developing architecture of identity and emotion. Although the system is still forming, the patterns established during this period can influence later interpretations and emotional responses.

As individuals move into adolescence, the architecture becomes more complex.

The mind begins interpreting experiences within a broader social and cultural context. Emotional responses intensify as individuals encounter new forms of independence, responsibility, and self-awareness. Identity becomes a central concern as adolescents begin asking who they are and how they fit within the world around them.

Meaning also expands during this period.

Young people begin exploring values, aspirations, and beliefs that extend beyond immediate circumstances. They experiment with different narratives about who they might become and what direction their lives might take. The architecture during this stage often involves significant exploration as individuals test interpretations and identities that may later evolve or change.

Early adulthood introduces another stage of development.

Responsibilities related to work, relationships, and personal independence require individuals to organize their psychological architecture in more stable ways. Interpretation begins focusing on practical decisions about career paths, partnerships, and long-term goals. Emotional responses become connected to commitments that carry lasting consequences.

Identity often becomes more defined during this period.

Individuals begin shaping narratives about who they are in relation to the roles they occupy. They may see themselves as professionals, partners, parents, creators, or contributors within a larger community. Meaning becomes connected to the pursuit of goals that extend across years rather than moments.

Yet the architecture continues evolving.

As individuals move through the middle years of life, they often encounter experiences that invite reconsideration of earlier assumptions. Successes and setbacks accumulate, relationships deepen or change, and priorities may shift as individuals reflect on what truly matters.

These experiences often prompt a reevaluation of identity and meaning.

A career that once defined a person's sense of purpose may begin to feel less central as other aspects of life gain importance. Values that once appeared secondary may become more significant. Interpretation begins adjusting to reflect the accumulated experience of years spent navigating the complexities of life.

Later stages of life bring additional transformations within the architecture.

Individuals often become more reflective about the narratives through which they understand their lives. Emotional responses may soften as the perspective gained through decades of experience provides a broader understanding of human behavior and relationships.

Identity may become less tied to specific roles and more connected to enduring aspects of the self.

Meaning may shift toward legacy, contribution, and the desire to share knowledge or support others. The architecture of experience begins integrating the many chapters of a life into a coherent narrative that reflects both struggle and growth.

Seen across a lifetime, the architecture of experience reveals itself as a continuously evolving system.

The same domains of interpretation, emotion, identity, and meaning remain present throughout life, yet the patterns through which they interact change as individuals encounter new experiences and perspectives.

This long view also reminds us that psychological growth does not belong to any single stage of life.

Individuals may encounter moments of transformation in youth, in midlife, or later in life when reflection becomes deeper. The architecture remains capable of reorganizing itself whenever individuals engage with experience in ways that introduce new understanding.

In this sense, the psychological system remains open to development across the entire course of human life.

Each stage offers opportunities to reinterpret past experiences, integrate emotional understanding, expand identity narratives, and reconnect with values that guide the direction of life.

The architecture continues evolving as long as life itself continues unfolding.

The Quiet Clarity of Understanding

When individuals begin recognizing the architecture through which their experience unfolds, the result is often less dramatic than people expect. There is rarely a single moment when life suddenly becomes easy or completely understandable. The structure of human experience remains complex, and uncertainty continues to accompany many of life's most meaningful decisions.

Yet something important changes.

Understanding the architecture introduces a quiet form of clarity into psychological life. Situations that once felt confusing may begin to make more sense when individuals can see how interpretation, emotion, identity, and meaning interact beneath the surface. Emotional responses that once appeared overwhelming may be understood as signals emerging from a system attempting to interpret experience and respond to it.

This clarity does not remove emotion.

Anger still arises when a boundary feels violated. Anxiety still appears when uncertainty increases. Sadness still emerges when loss becomes unavoidable. These emotional responses remain part of the architecture of human life, and they continue serving the regulatory functions that make psychological experience possible.

What changes is the relationship individuals have with these responses.

Instead of feeling completely defined by the emotions of the moment, individuals begin recognizing how those emotions fit within a larger system. They understand that emotional responses are connected to interpretations of experience, that identity narratives influence how those interpretations form, and that meaning shapes the direction in which the system moves.

Through this understanding, emotional experiences often become easier to navigate.

The individual may still feel anger, but they can ask what interpretation produced the emotion. They may still experience anxiety, but they can explore whether their interpretation of the situation reflects the full reality of what is happening. They may feel sadness, yet recognize that the emotion reflects something meaningful within their life.

This perspective allows emotional life to become more integrated.

The architecture no longer appears chaotic or unpredictable. Instead, individuals begin seeing how their psychological system attempts to organize experience through patterns that reflect both past learning and present interpretation.

Identity also becomes clearer.

When people understand how identity narratives form and evolve, they may feel less pressure to defend a rigid story about who they are. The narrative of the self can remain open to revision as new experiences appear. Individuals become more willing to integrate complexity into their understanding of themselves.

Meaning becomes more stable as well.

Instead of relying solely on specific achievements or circumstances to provide purpose, individuals begin connecting their sense of meaning to values that can endure across changing conditions. Even when life introduces difficulty or uncertainty, those values continue providing orientation within the architecture of experience.

The clarity that emerges from this understanding is therefore not a form of certainty.

It is a form of orientation.

Individuals recognize the processes through which their experiences are interpreted, regulated, and integrated. They understand that psychological life involves ongoing interaction among the domains that shape human experience. Instead of searching for permanent answers, they learn to navigate the system with greater awareness.

This awareness often brings a quiet sense of steadiness.

Difficult moments no longer feel completely disorienting because the individual understands how the architecture responds to challenge. Emotional responses are recognized as part of a system that can process and integrate experience. Identity remains capable of evolving, and meaning continues guiding the direction of life.

Over time, this understanding can deepen a person's relationship with both themselves and the world around them.

Individuals become more attentive to the interpretations they form, more respectful of the emotional signals they experience, more flexible in the narratives they carry about themselves, and more thoughtful about the values that shape their sense of purpose.

The architecture of being human remains complex.

Yet when individuals begin seeing that architecture clearly, psychological life becomes less mysterious and more understandable. The system through which human experience unfolds reveals itself not as something to control or eliminate, but as something to understand and inhabit more fully.

And within that understanding, a quiet clarity begins to emerge.

* * *

10

The Future of Psychological Architecture

sychological frameworks often begin with the promise that if we understand ourselves well enough, the confusion of human experience will eventually give way to clarity. Yet by the time readers reach the end of this book, it should be clear that understanding the architecture of the mind does not simplify life in that way. Human experience remains complex, emotional life remains powerful, and identity continues evolving as circumstances change.

What understanding does offer is orientation.

Throughout this book we have examined the structure through which human experience unfolds. The mind interprets the world and attempts to organize events into patterns that make sense. Emotion responds to those interpretations, signaling what matters and motivating action. Identity gathers those experiences into the narrative through which individuals understand who they are. Meaning connects that narrative to values and direction, allowing life to feel oriented toward something larger than the moment itself.

These domains do not operate separately.

They interact constantly, shaping the patterns through which people respond to challenges, relationships, and the unfolding course of their lives. Much of the confusion people experience about their own reactions arises not because the system is chaotic, but because its structure usually remains

154

invisible.

Once the structure becomes visible, psychological life begins to look different.

Experiences that once appeared unpredictable often reveal patterns of interpretation and emotional response. Identity struggles that once felt deeply personal may reflect the system's attempt to maintain coherence during periods of change. Moments when meaning seems to disappear may signal the need to reconnect life with values that provide direction.

Understanding the architecture does not eliminate difficulty, but it changes how individuals encounter it.

Instead of feeling as though emotions or reactions emerge without explanation, people can begin recognizing the processes that give rise to them. Interpretation can be examined. Emotional responses can be understood as signals rather than problems. Identity narratives can be expanded rather than defended. Meaning can be rediscovered when life begins to feel disoriented.

In this way, the framework of Psychological Architecture is less about solving the problem of being human and more about understanding the structure through which human experience unfolds.

When individuals begin seeing that structure clearly, they gain a different relationship with their own psychological life. The system through which they experience the world becomes something they can observe, understand, and engage with more consciously.

The future of Psychological Architecture lies in this shift of perspective.

It invites us to see human experience not as a series of isolated thoughts, emotions, or behaviors, but as an integrated system through which interpretation, emotion, identity, and meaning continually interact. Through that lens, the complexity of human life becomes not something to eliminate, but something to understand.

And within that understanding, a deeper clarity about what it means to be human begins to emerge.

Reframing Psychological Inquiry

For much of its modern history, psychology has approached the human mind by separating its components. Researchers study cognition, emotion, personality, development, motivation, and social behavior as distinct areas of inquiry. Each of these domains has produced valuable insights about particular aspects of psychological functioning. Yet the lived experience of being human rarely appears in such neatly separated categories.

In everyday life, thought and emotion are inseparable. Emotional responses shape interpretation, and interpretation influences emotion in return. Identity provides the narrative through which individuals understand their experiences across time, while meaning connects those experiences to values that guide decisions and effort. Human experience therefore unfolds not as a collection of isolated processes, but as a system in which these elements interact continuously.

Psychological Architecture invites a shift in how psychological life is understood.

Rather than beginning with isolated processes and attempting to assemble them afterward, the framework begins with the structure of experience itself. Interpretation, emotion, identity, and meaning are not treated as separate psychological topics. They are understood as domains within a single architecture that organizes how human beings encounter the world.

From this perspective, many familiar psychological phenomena appear in a new light.

Anxiety, for example, can be understood not only as an emotional state but as the result of particular interpretations interacting with the emotional regulatory system. Identity struggles may reflect tensions within the narratives individuals use to organize their experiences across time. Loss of meaning may occur when the system's values no longer provide direction for interpretation and action.

When these elements are examined together, psychological life becomes easier to understand as a dynamic system.

This reframing does not diminish the importance of the many specialized fields within psychology. Cognitive research continues to reveal how the mind processes information. Affective science deepens our understanding of emotional regulation. Developmental psychology explores how individuals change across the lifespan.

Psychological Architecture instead offers a conceptual lens through which these insights can be integrated.

By focusing on the interactions among interpretation, emotion, identity, and meaning, the framework highlights how different psychological processes combine to shape lived experience. This perspective helps explain why individuals often feel caught in repeating patterns. It also clarifies how change becomes possible when one domain begins interacting differently with the others.

Reframing psychological inquiry in this way encourages researchers and practitioners to look not only at individual mechanisms, but also at the patterns that emerge from their interaction.

Understanding these patterns allows psychological life to be studied as a coherent system rather than as a set of disconnected phenomena. In doing so, the architecture of human experience becomes easier to recognize both in research and in the everyday lives of individuals.

Psychological Architecture as a Systems Framework

One of the central ideas running through this book is that human psychological life functions as a system. The experiences people have each day may appear fragmented or unpredictable, but beneath that surface lies an organized structure through which interpretation, emotion, identity, and meaning continually interact. Psychological Architecture attempts to describe that structure in a way that makes the dynamics of experience easier to recognize.

A systems framework begins from the assumption that individual elements cannot be fully understood in isolation.

In many areas of science, systems thinking has provided a way of understanding complex phenomena that arise from the interaction of multiple components. Biological systems depend on relationships among organs, cells, and regulatory processes. Ecological systems emerge from the interactions among organisms and their environments. In similar ways, psychological life unfolds through relationships among processes that shape how individuals interpret, feel, understand themselves, and pursue meaning.

When psychological processes are examined separately, their interactions can become difficult to see.

Thought may be studied without considering the emotional signals that influence interpretation. Emotional responses may be examined without fully exploring the identity narratives that shape how those responses are experienced. Identity may be discussed without examining the values and meanings that guide the direction of a person's life.

A systems perspective helps reconnect these elements.

Within Psychological Architecture, interpretation provides the system with explanations about what is happening in the world. Emotion regulates the intensity of the system's response to those interpretations. Identity organizes experience across time, creating continuity in the story individuals tell about themselves. Meaning connects that story to values that orient the individual toward future action.

Because these domains interact continuously, changes in one area often influence the entire system.

A shift in interpretation may reduce emotional reactivity. Emotional experiences that are processed rather than avoided may gradually reshape identity narratives. As identity evolves, individuals may discover new sources of meaning that influence how they interpret their circumstances and choose their actions.

These interactions illustrate how psychological change often occurs through adjustments within the system rather than through isolated interventions.

A person who learns to examine their interpretations more carefully may discover that emotional responses become easier to regulate. Someone who processes emotional experiences more openly may begin revising the identity narratives they once carried about themselves. As identity becomes more flexible, individuals may reconnect with values that restore meaning and direction in their lives.

Seen in this way, psychological growth reflects the gradual integration of the system.

Interpretation becomes more responsive to the complexity of experience. Emotional signals become part of a process of understanding rather than sources of disruption. Identity evolves to incorporate new experiences without losing coherence. Meaning continues orienting the individual toward values that guide effort and decision.

Psychological Architecture therefore offers more than a set of individual concepts.

It provides a framework for seeing how the different elements of psychological life form an organized structure. This structure is not rigid or mechanical. It evolves as individuals encounter new experiences, reinterpret their past, and adjust their values in response to changing circumstances.

By viewing psychological life as a system, the architecture becomes easier to understand.

The patterns that once appeared confusing begin to reveal the relationships among interpretation, emotion, identity, and meaning. Through this perspective, the complexity of human experience becomes not something chaotic, but something structured and intelligible.Psychological Architecture as a Systems Framework

One of the central ideas running through this book is that human psychological life functions as a system. The experiences people have each day may appear fragmented or unpredictable, but beneath that surface lies an organized structure through which interpretation, emotion, identity, and meaning continually interact. Psychological Architecture attempts to describe that structure in a way that makes the dynamics of experience easier to recognize.

A systems framework begins from the assumption that individual elements cannot be fully understood in isolation.

In many areas of science, systems thinking has provided a way of understanding complex phenomena that arise from the interaction of multiple components. Biological systems depend on relationships among organs, cells, and regulatory processes. Ecological systems emerge from the interactions among organisms and their environments. In similar ways, psychological life unfolds through relationships among processes that shape how individuals interpret, feel, understand themselves, and pursue meaning.

When psychological processes are examined separately, their interactions can become difficult to see.

Thought may be studied without considering the emotional signals that influence interpretation. Emotional responses may be examined without fully exploring the identity narratives that shape how those responses are experienced. Identity may be discussed without examining the values and meanings that guide the direction of a person's life.

A systems perspective helps reconnect these elements.

Within Psychological Architecture, interpretation provides the system with explanations about what is happening in the world. Emotion regulates the intensity of the system's response to those interpretations. Identity organizes experience across time, creating continuity in the story individuals tell about themselves. Meaning connects that story to values that orient the individual toward future action.

Because these domains interact continuously, changes in one area often influence the entire system.

A shift in interpretation may reduce emotional reactivity. Emotional experiences that are processed rather than avoided may gradually reshape identity narratives. As identity evolves, individuals may discover new sources of meaning that influence how they interpret their circumstances and choose their actions.

These interactions illustrate how psychological change often occurs through adjustments within the system rather than through isolated interventions.

A person who learns to examine their interpretations more carefully may discover that emotional responses become easier to regulate. Someone who processes emotional experiences more openly may begin revising the identity narratives they once carried about themselves. As identity becomes more flexible, individuals may reconnect with values that restore meaning and direction in their lives.

Seen in this way, psychological growth reflects the gradual integration of the system.

Interpretation becomes more responsive to the complexity of experience. Emotional signals become part of a process of understanding rather than sources of disruption. Identity evolves to incorporate new experiences without losing coherence. Meaning continues orienting the individual toward values that guide effort and decision.

Psychological Architecture therefore offers more than a set of individual concepts.

It provides a framework for seeing how the different elements of psychological life form an organized structure. This structure is not rigid or mechanical. It evolves as individuals encounter new experiences, reinterpret their past, and adjust their values in response to changing circumstances.

By viewing psychological life as a system, the architecture becomes easier to understand.

The patterns that once appeared confusing begin to reveal the relationships among interpretation, emotion, identity, and meaning. Through this perspective, the complexity of human experience becomes not something chaotic, but something structured and intelligible.

Implications for Research and Practice

If human psychological experience is organized through the interaction of interpretation, emotion, identity, and meaning, then understanding psychological life requires attention to how these domains function together. This perspective carries implications not only for individuals seeking to understand themselves, but also for the broader ways psychology studies and responds to human experience.

A structural perspective also opens several directions for future inquiry. Psychological research has often examined interpretation, emotion, identity, and meaning as separate domains of study. A structural framework invites investigation into how these domains interact dynamically within the organization of experience. Future research may increasingly explore how interpretive patterns influence emotional regulation, how emotional experience shapes identity development, and how meaning frameworks influence long-term psychological stability.

Clinical work may also benefit from a structural perspective. Many forms of distress are often approached through the treatment of individual symptoms such as anxiety, rumination, or emotional dysregulation. A structural view suggests that such experiences may reflect tensions distributed across several domains simultaneously. Emotional distress may arise not only from immediate circumstances but also from interpretive habits, identity vulnerabilities, and disruptions in meaning. Understanding these interactions may allow psychological intervention to address the broader architecture of experience rather than focusing solely on isolated symptoms.

Educational approaches to psychology may likewise benefit from structural integration. Students are often introduced to psychological knowledge through highly specialized domains that appear only loosely connected. A structural framework provides a way of organizing these insights within a coherent map of human experience. By examining how interpretation, emotion, identity, and meaning operate together, psychology can be taught not only as a collection of findings but also as an integrated understanding of how psychological life unfolds.

Research in psychology has often produced deep insight into particular mechanisms of the mind. Studies of cognitive processing reveal how individuals interpret information and form beliefs. Research in affective science explores the mechanisms through which emotions arise and influence behavior. Developmental psychology examines how identity evolves across the lifespan. Work in motivation and well-being investigates how meaning and purpose influence human flourishing.

Each of these fields illuminates an important dimension of psychological life.

Yet when these areas are examined independently, the broader structure through which experience unfolds can remain partially obscured. Psychological Architecture suggests that a more complete understanding emerges when these domains are studied as interacting components within a system.

For research, this perspective encourages questions that cross traditional boundaries.

How do patterns of interpretation influence emotional regulation over time? In what ways do emotional experiences shape the narratives individuals construct about themselves? How does identity influence the kinds of meanings individuals pursue, and how do those meanings in turn reshape identity?

These kinds of questions focus less on isolated processes and more on the relationships among them.

Examining these interactions may help researchers better understand why certain psychological patterns persist, why some individuals adapt to change more easily than others, and how shifts in one area of psychological life influence broader patterns of behavior and experience.

The implications extend beyond research into the ways psychological knowledge is applied in everyday life.

In therapeutic settings, individuals often seek help for experiences that feel confusing or overwhelming. Emotional distress, identity uncertainty, or loss of meaning may appear as separate problems. Yet these experiences frequently arise through interactions among the different domains of psychological life.

Viewing these challenges through the lens of Psychological Architecture can provide a broader context for understanding them.

Anxiety may reflect patterns of interpretation interacting with emotional regulation. Identity struggles may arise when new experiences challenge the narratives individuals have carried about themselves. Loss of meaning may emerge when existing values no longer provide direction in changing circumstances.

Recognizing these interactions allows individuals to approach psychological change more holistically.

Rather than focusing exclusively on a single symptom or behavior, attention can shift toward understanding how interpretations, emotional responses, identity narratives, and sources of meaning interact within the broader system. Adjustments within one domain may gradually influence the others, creating space for new patterns of experience.

In everyday life, this perspective also invites individuals to observe their own psychological processes with greater curiosity.

Moments of emotional intensity can be examined as signals about interpretations and values rather than simply as problems to eliminate. Identity narratives can be reconsidered as evolving stories rather than fixed definitions of the self. Experiences that challenge existing meanings may become opportunities to clarify what matters most.

Through this lens, psychological life becomes something that can be understood as it unfolds.

The architecture does not remove the complexity of being human, but it provides a framework through which that complexity becomes more intelligible. Interpretation, emotion, identity, and meaning remain deeply intertwined, continually shaping how individuals encounter the world and understand themselves within it.

Living Within the Architecture of Being Human

By the time readers reach the end of this book, one idea should have become increasingly clear: human experience is not random. The patterns through which people interpret events, respond emotionally, understand who they are, and pursue meaning are not scattered fragments of mental activity. They form a structure.

That structure is what this book has called Psychological Architecture.

Recognizing this architecture does not mean reducing human life to a mechanical system. People remain complex, emotional, creative, and deeply shaped by the circumstances of their lives. Relationships remain unpredictable. Personal growth continues to unfold through challenges that cannot always be anticipated or controlled.

What changes is the way those experiences are understood.

When individuals begin to see the architecture beneath their experiences, the confusion that often accompanies psychological life becomes easier to navigate. Emotional reactions that once felt overwhelming can be recognized as signals emerging from the interaction between interpretation and emotional regulation. Identity struggles can be understood as moments when the narrative of the self is adjusting to new experiences. Loss of meaning can be seen not as a failure of character, but as an indication that values and direction may need to be reconsidered.

In this way, the architecture offers orientation.

Rather than attempting to control every thought or emotion, individuals can begin observing how their psychological system operates. Interpretations can be examined with greater awareness. Emotional responses can be approached with curiosity rather than immediate judgment. Identity can be recognized as a narrative that evolves as new experiences are integrated. Meaning can be rediscovered when individuals reconnect with the values that give their lives direction.

Living within this architecture does not require mastering the system completely.

No person maintains perfect clarity about their interpretations or emotions at every moment. Identity continues evolving throughout life. Meaning may shift as circumstances change and new experiences reshape the direction of a person's life.

What matters is the ability to recognize the structure through which these experiences unfold.

When individuals understand that their thoughts, emotions, identity, and sense of meaning form an interacting system, they gain a different relationship with their psychological lives. Reactions that once appeared mysterious begin to reveal patterns. Difficult moments can be approached as part of the system's ongoing effort to adapt and reorganize itself.

Through this perspective, psychological life becomes something that can be engaged with more consciously.

Individuals can pause to examine the interpretations guiding their reactions. They can listen more carefully to emotional signals rather than immediately attempting to suppress them. They can reconsider identity narratives that may have become too rigid to accommodate new experiences. They can return to the question of meaning when life begins to feel disoriented.

These small shifts gradually change how people inhabit their own lives.

The architecture remains present whether it is recognized or not. The mind continues interpreting experience. Emotion continues signaling what matters. Identity continues organizing the story of the self. Meaning continues orienting individuals toward the values that shape their lives.

Yet when this structure becomes visible, individuals are no longer moving through their experiences blindly.

They begin to see the patterns shaping their reactions, relationships, and decisions. The complexity of human life remains, but it becomes more intelligible. What once felt chaotic begins to reveal the underlying structure through which experience unfolds.

In this sense, Psychological Architecture is not merely a framework for understanding the mind.

Understanding the architecture of being human does not eliminate the complexity of life. It clarifies the structure within which that complexity unfolds.

* * *

The framework described in this book should therefore be understood as an initial articulation rather than a final statement. Psychological Architecture proposes one way of examining how interpretation, emotion, identity, and meaning interact to organize human experience. As with any structural perspective, its value will ultimately depend on how well it helps illuminate patterns that might otherwise remain difficult to see. Future research, dialogue, and application will refine, challenge, and expand this framework over time. The architecture described here is therefore not a finished structure but an invitation to ongoing inquiry into the organization of psychological life.

About the Author

RJ Starr is a psychology educator, writer, and independent scholar whose work explores the structure of human experience. He is the creator of Psychological Architecture, a conceptual framework that organizes psychological life around four interacting domains: mind, emotion, identity, and meaning. Through his writing, lectures, and public scholarship, Starr seeks to make complex psychological ideas accessible without sacrificing intellectual depth.

He is the author of several books on human behavior, perception, and personal narrative, including *The Psychology of Being Human: An Authoritative Guide to Mind, Emotion, and Meaning*. His work examines how individuals interpret their lives, construct identity, regulate emotion, and pursue meaning in a rapidly changing world.

RJ Starr publishes essays, research, and educational material through his platform at profrjstarr.com, where his work continues to develop the ideas introduced in this book.

You can connect with me on:

🌐 https://profrjstarr.com
🐦 https://x.com/profrjstarr
📘 https://www.facebook.com/profrjstarr